YOUR
MANIFESTING
YEAR

YOUR

MANIFESTING

YEAR

Joey Hulin

Published by Sourcebooks
P.O. Box 4410, Naperville, Illinois 60567-4410
(630) 961-3900
sourcebooks.com

Originally published in 2022 in Great Britain by Ebury Press, an imprint of Ebury Publishing. Ebury Press is part of the Penguin Random House group of companies whose addresses can be found at global.penguinrandomhouse.com

Cataloging-in-Publication Data is on file with the Library of Congress.

Printed and bound in the United States of America.
POD

CONTENTS

A NOTE FOR READERS

Some of the spells in this book use candles. Never leave a burning candle unattended.

INTRODUCTION

Are you ready to embark on a year of magic, synchronicity, deep inner healing and feeling great, all while manifesting your desires into reality? Over the course of a year, you will discover how simple mindset shifts, practices and intentions can help you manifest your desires, and feel great in the process. Each month we will explore different themes and practices, from starting the new year by manifesting luck, to love, community, abundance, self-acceptance and so much more.

WHAT IS MANIFESTING?

Manifesting is a magical practice where science and mysticism meet, involving an exploration of your relationship with yourself and with the universe. In order to consciously 'manifest' something, your thoughts, subconscious beliefs, words, actions, behaviours, habits, somatic body and your inner wisdom have to be in alignment. You have to *be* the true expression of yourself. And here's the thing – it shouldn't feel like 'work' or something you have to strive towards – instead, it is something you will relax into. If it feels joyful, intriguing, light, enjoyable and like a full-body state of trust and surrender, then you've nailed it! The universe responds to your vibration if: you're clear on what you want; you have absolute trust that it will show up when the time is right; you take conscious, joyful action every day towards it; and you find appreciation in the ever-unfolding journey. Then, magic will happen!

Manifesting requires you to lift the lid on your dreams and to let yourself truly want what you want. Setting intentions is like lighting a beacon of hope and lining up the starting blocks so you're heading in the right direction. Each month we will look at how to set intentions, to embody your desires in the here and now, and fall in love with the journey unfolding. The more present you are in each step, the more likely you'll be able to notice the synchronicities and signs laid out for you along the way.

One thing is for certain – you won't manifest your desires through dreaming alone, when sitting at home waiting for something to come to you. You have to participate in this life, and take soul-aligned actions and risks. So well done for picking up this book!

This year is *your* opportunity to really let yourself claim what it is that you want to experience during your one precious, miraculous life. I will be cheering you on in each chapter to take conscious steps towards your desires, while also guiding you to do the inner work, to unblock what is holding you back from experiencing it all. Manifesting is about internal shifts that lead to confidence and belief in yourself in the now, a greater sense of hope for the future, and an ability to offer a greater contribution to the world.

In each chapter we will explore different theories and practices to help bring all this to life. You will find practical things to try, and you can work through them at your own pace throughout the month. You will explore your mindset and beliefs, vibration, visualisation, symbols, rituals, spells, meditations and much more. But before you dive into your first chapter, let's take a brief look at each of these and why they are important when manifesting.

Your mindset and beliefs

As you will explore throughout the year, your mindset has a huge impact on just about everything in your life, including your ability to manifest your desires. Thoughts that are practised over and over become your beliefs. Those beliefs are either in alignment with what you truly want, or they may be holding you back. In order to attract what you want into your life, your thoughts must be in alignment with your desires because, according to the law of attraction, thoughts attract things, as you will explore in the August chapter, on abundance.

The thoughts we think affect the chemistry of our bodies. Serotonin is created when we experience positive emotions, and cortisol (the stress hormone) is decreased. Practices such as mindfulness and meditation help you become aware of your thought patterns and gradually 'rewire' the neural pathways in the brain. Gratitude and affirmations are go-to practices to help facilitate positive change, and they are essential practices when manifesting too, which is why you will find them as tools to use throughout the year.

Your vibration

We live in a vibrational universe. Everything is a vibration, from the sounds you hear to the emotions you feel. This emotional energy is so potent that most people are able to feel it outside of themselves. Have you ever entered a room after two people have been fighting and you could sense the tension in the air? Science confirms that energy vibrating at a certain frequency will attract energy vibrating at the same frequency, just like a magnet. So, when you feel the emotions associated with your desire, you attract more of what you desire. But you can't fool the universe or your subconscious mind by pretending you feel good when in truth you feel rubbish. Instead, tend compassionately and lovingly to what it is that feels hurt, fearful or out of alignment in order to raise your vibration, even just slightly. We will look at ways to feel good and 'raise your vibration' throughout the book.

Say it out loud

Once you are clear on what you want – claim it! Get clear on exactly what you want to experience each month, then ask for it! Say it out loud, post it on social media, tell your best friend, be bold and brave. Use positive language and state what is going to happen, along with the actions you'll be taking. Ask the universe for what you want, take action, and then watch for signs and synchronicities to appear to assist you, and have fun with it!

Visualisations

When you visualise, the idea is to evoke the feeling of your desire from within, to embody the frequency of your desire here and now. It's not about trying to 'manipulate' the external world. You visualise to vibrate at the frequency of your desires and to feel good in the present moment. This, practised over the course of a year, will help you to embody your desires, therefore increasing the chances of your physical reality matching up.

Neuroscientists have proven that the same area of the brain is activated when you are imagining an image and when you are looking at the real thing. Visualising something evokes the same feelings, chemicals and energetic vibration as if you already have it! Visualisation even impacts your muscle memory. Savour and delight in the visualisations you are offered in this book. Indulge your imagination and creativity in the dream and then hand it over to the universe. At the end of a visualisation, you return fully to the present moment, because it is only here and now where you truly experience life. This is how you keep your vibe high – it's about how you feel now, not waiting for some future day to come.

Symbols, talismans and totems

Symbols are the language of the unconscious mind. A symbol can be pretty much anything that means something to you. In each chapter I give you some ideas for symbols that you can draw, wear or have in your home to help you focus on the theme of the month. Symbols can convey a spiritual meaning and act as communication between the conscious and unconscious mind. Symbols can also be interpreted as information and messages from the universe, perhaps through dreams, or seeing repetitive numbers or shapes, especially when you have asked for guidance. Symbols have been used in this way since ancient times, from ancient Egypt to pre-Roman Britain. The more present you are, the easier it will be to notice if symbols and signs are jumping out at you and hold meaning for you along the way.

My suggestion is to have one symbol each month that represents your intention, and to keep them somewhere safe throughout the year. At the end of the year, compile them on a vision board or pinboard, or stick them in a mandala shape in a journal to keep the magic you have been weaving throughout the year alive.

In some chapters you will also discover talismans and totems. These are objects said to hold magical powers or to bring about good luck. It might be an object worn, held or displayed somewhere of significance. Again, I suggest keeping these to hand, perhaps in your pocket, wearing them or keeping them on an altar at home to help ground your intentions as you journey through each month.

Meditations

Meditation is the absolute foundation to all spiritual practices, especially manifesting. If there is one thing that will change just about every aspect of your life for the better, when you show up to practise it, it is meditation.

A simple, short, daily meditation practice can help regulate your emotions; reduce stress and anxiety; improve sleep, focus and compassion; and heighten the experience of natural awe, mindfulness and presence, alongside a whole host of other neurological, physical and emotional benefits. Manifesting works best when our nervous system is regulated and you are present, relaxed and in alignment, and meditation will help you do that. I include meditation moments in each chapter and you can find guided recordings of them on Spotify or via @joeyhuin_writer on Instagram to help you along your way.

Rituals, ceremonies and spells

Rituals, ceremonies and spells are about playing with and directing energy in order to manifest your desires. Meditation often plays a part in these too, because it helps you get focused, and stay focused, as you perform your spells.

Rituals are intentional practices consciously performed and set aside from the daily routine. They are often performed to integrate body and mind and arouse emotions. Much like visualisations, the energy and focus of spells and rituals is to be contained within the practice, and then surrendered to the universe. Pagan rituals will often encourage practitioners to ground themselves, and dismantle any altars or circles created for the practice, so as to fully integrate back into the physical world and the present moment. We will do that at several points throughout the book.

New moons and the waxing moon phase leading up to a full moon are potent times to cast spells, as a new moon symbolises new beginnings. The full moon and a waning moon symbolise release and letting go. I explain each month when it is best to perform the spells in the book, but it is you the practitioner that holds the power, so when it truly works for you is best.

SMUDGING

Burning dried sage, and other herbs, is often referred to as 'smudging'. This is done to cleanse the energy of a room, an object or a person's energy field. Burning white sage is a sacred practice in Native American cultures, while using cleansing smoke, burning herbs and incense has been practised all over the world in many traditions, including paganism.

You will be instructed to perform this cleansing ritual at various times throughout the year. You will need a bundle of dried sage, known as a smudging stick. Make sure you open windows if you are cleansing an indoor space with smoke, and safely stub out any embers when you have finished.

How to use this book

No matter which month you bought this book, start right there. You might like to read the chapter in full at the start of the month, then check the moon cycles online to make a plan for when and where you will perform the ritual or spell. There are plenty of things you can do right now, too. Make a conscious decision at the start of each month to approach the themes with a beginner's mind and an open heart.

I encourage you to keep a note of any synchronicities, magical occurrences, signs and spiritual nudges that you experience each month. It is so easy to forget them when they occur and by keeping track in a journal or notebook, you might notice patterns. It can be encouraging and rewarding to look back on all the magic you have experienced once the year is complete.

In every moment you are being reborn. Every thought or action you make and take is either in the direction of manifesting your desires, or circling back to the past. Thoughts are either in resonance with your desires, or they are drawing you away from it. With manifesting, the less you try to control or force an outcome, the quicker you will receive it!

When it feels like nothing is changing . . .

Starting a manifesting practice doesn't mean you will switch from one state to another in the blink of an eye – from lingering sadness to consistent joy, or from being broke to being a millionaire, for example. Sometimes, leaps do take place when your desire manifests quickly, but more often than not, these things take time, especially when there is deep inner healing taking place. Personal learning, growth and evolution is a lifelong process. The trick is to enjoy the process and find it fascinating, no matter the pace.

This book is for you

Although we live in a metaphysical, energetic world, we also live in a very human one, governed by collective beliefs, biases, prejudices and unequal organisational structures. For that reason, I would like to acknowledge that it is unquestionably easier for some people to get a head start when manifesting certain things, because of their gender, skin colour, background or social status. Many societies are built on outdated, toxic, colonialist and patriarchal beliefs. These very real injustices undoubtedly affords some privileges and shortcuts on a practical level, but on a metaphysical level we are all the same, and all have equal potential to manifest changes. The manifesting practices you will find in this book are for those who believe in bringing balance and harmony to masculine and feminine energies in the world, and to ensure equal opportunities for all. This book is especially for those who identify with marginalised or downtrodden groups, and individuals who dream of a better life and a fairer world for themselves, their families and communities, and the earth, no matter their background.

Everything we manifest has an impact on other people, the planet and the future, as you will explore in December's chapter. Therefore, this book is about being conscious, holistic and altruistic manifestors, not just materialistic ones. The practices you'll find in this book are offered to help you, no matter where you are in life or what circumstances you currently find yourself in, because you deserve it. Manifesting is about intention, action, resilience, belief and, most of all, it is about having fun. When you are the most aligned version of yourself, you will feel great, you will be magnetic and there will be no stopping you.

So, are you ready to create some magic?

01

LUCK

JANUARY

'PAUSE BEFORE THIS NEW YEAR BEGINS, AS YOU CROSS THE THRESHOLD INTO A NEW YEAR OF ENDLESS POSSIBILITIES'

s luck something that happens to us? Is it a force greater than the human self, something we have no control over? Or is it something that we can influence – and if so, how?

The start of a new calendar year brings with it a potency of potential. Whether you are deep in the winter in the northern hemisphere or in the height of summer in the southern hemisphere, the new year offers you an opportunity to pause, reflect and redirect. January often gets a bad rap in the northern hemisphere, thanks to the cold, dark days and the stillness after a busy festive season. However, I believe January offers a chance for a beautiful, reflective time while you consider the direction of travel you are going in this year, and what it is you want to manifest. Forget setting resolutions which aren't sustainable and don't bring you joy. Instead, consciously pause before this new year begins, as you cross the threshold into a new year of endless possibilities. Let this year be your manifesting year.

So, what exactly is luck?

There are many opposing views on this. According to several dictionary definitions, luck is a force that we have no control over, a result of fate which is out of our hands. Yet according to some spiritual teachers and psychologists, luck is something we have agency over, and so we can manifest more of it in our lives. An article published in the *Harvard Business Review* by Morten T. Hansen claimed corporate luck can be influenced by recognising luck when it occurs; being prepared for and accepting of bad luck as part of the process; and being ready to respond effectively when good luck arrives. A ten-year study, by psychologist Richard Wiseman at the University of Hertfordshire, concluded that lucky people do create their own luck, mostly by noticing opportunities and expecting good things to happen, so luck becomes a self-fulfilling prophecy. His study concludes that listening to your intuition and being resilient to the inevitable bad luck that we all experience from time to time is the key.

We might consider something to be a result of luck when the unexpected happens, such as a chance meeting or a perfect opportunity presenting itself out of the blue. Or perhaps when we experience a near miss, dodging what might have been considered a 'bad luck' experience.

Luck can also be considered to be an attribute, with people self-proclaiming to be either a 'lucky' or an 'unlucky' person. We often find luck and superstition come hand in hand, where small rituals are performed or good luck charms are carried, in order to ward off bad luck and to draw in the good.

I like to think of luck and manifesting as interlinked.They are both fulfilled through 'synchronicity', an energetic law that activates when there is a clear communication between our inner desires and outer actions. We can also think of manifesting luck as simply mindfulness in disguise. Starting the new year exploring your relationship with luck is setting a firm foundation for manifesting throughout the year, because you are deepening your relationship with synchronicity. As your dreams start to manifest throughout the year, some people might say to you 'How lucky!', while you will know that luck is the embodiment of mindset, presence and divine timing.

DO YOU FEEL LUCKY?

Exploring your own personal beliefs regarding luck is vital when considering how to manifest more of it into your life. Spend some time in quiet reflection and journal your answers to the following prompts. Allow your answers to pour onto the page as a stream of consciousness, unedited and answered quickly, without judgement.

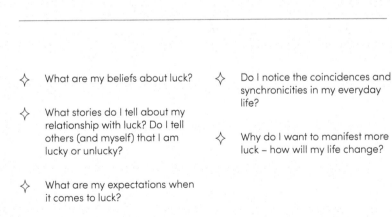

✧ What are my beliefs about luck?

✧ What stories do I tell about my relationship with luck? Do I tell others (and myself) that I am lucky or unlucky?

✧ What are my expectations when it comes to luck?

✧ Do I notice the coincidences and synchronicities in my everyday life?

✧ Why do I want to manifest more luck – how will my life change?

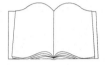

A STORY OF MANIFESTING LUCK

In 2013, the band Mumford & Sons headlined Glastonbury Festival. Mega fan and up-and-coming singer-songwriter Sian Cross was a festival goer that year and eagerly awaited their set. As luck would have it, the band who were scheduled to play directly before Mumford & Sons had the same manager as Sian. Her manager called her just before Mumford & Sons were due to go on the Pyramid Stage with the news that she'd been able to get hold of side-of-stage passes for them both. They took their places and watched the whole set in elation. For their final song, Mumford & Sons played Joe Cocker's song 'With A Little Help From My Friends', which was Sian's dad's favourite song and the song that was played at his funeral. Sian recalled in an interview how she felt so lucky that day, and saw it as a sign from the universe, and her dad, to keep going with her music. It wasn't until she got home the next day that she realised the extra layer of magic. In amazement, she stood looking at a vision board she had created months earlier. Alongside a photo of the Pyramid Stage, there was one of Mumford & Sons, and dancing along the bottom of the board, in playful writing, was the line 'I get by with a little help from my friends.'

Change your mind

We are always in a state of manifesting. Every thought we have, every choice, action and response we make, shapes the reality in which we live – either consciously or unconsciously. We are master manifestors without even realising! A deliberate, conscious manifesting practice enables us to shape the direction of our day, our year and our life. Paradoxically, luck can be a result of forces outside of our control, but it is equally something we have agency over, and we can achieve this through some simple shifts in mindset.

Spiritual teacher Deepak Chopra suggests in his book *Synchrodestiny* (1998) that luck is a result of opportunity and preparedness coming together. He reminds us that having a very clear intention is the key to recognising opportunities but, crucially, you need to act when an opportunity arises.

So, how do we recognise opportunities, and how do we prepare for them throughout the year? Opportunities present themselves to us every single day. Having a clear intention is how we filter the information to notice these opportunities. The best way for us to 'prepare' for receiving good luck is to be present, mindful and aware throughout our day-to-day life – essentially, to practise mindfulness. Being fully present and aware is the best way to notice the 'coincidences', the serendipitous signs and clues, laid out by the universe along our path like little breadcrumbs for us to follow. Mindfulness also brings about more self-awareness, and through self-knowledge we are able to become conscious of the stories we tell ourselves, and others, about our own identification with luck. This will form the foundation for all manifesting practices we will explore throughout this year.

DECIDE TO BE LUCKY

What if you started to believe and affirm that you are lucky? How different might this year feel if you start to believe in synchronicity and divine guidance, the very substance of luck? We can practise repeating positive affirmations in order to alchemise our internal beliefs. Repeat the following affirmations out loud each morning to yourself in the mirror. Make it easy to form the habit by writing them on a sticky note and placing them on your bathroom mirror. Try this just before or after brushing your teeth!

✧ I am a lucky person

✧ I invite magical experiences and synchronicity into this day

✧ I am naturally lucky

✧ Every day, I attract more good things into my life

✧ I co-create luck with the universe

✧ This year, I choose to be lucky

A SPELL FOR
GOOD LUCK

A new moon is the start of a new lunar cycle and it symbolises new beginnings. It is a potent time to set new intentions or to call in all that you desire. This month, we are going to play with a spell, but remember, the real power in any spell is the focused intention brought to it by you, the practitioner.

There is an old English tradition for good luck, in which fishermen bought or were gifted a 'witch's ladder' to bring them good luck before a lengthy trip at sea. A witch's ladder is a long piece of string or thin rope with knots, feathers or charms tied into it, created to draw in good luck. This spell is based on that idea, but you are going to create your own witch's ladder throughout this month.

You will need

A piece of string (or thin rope or wool),
at least 30 cm (12 in) long

The practice

1   Start your practice as early into the month as you can. Loop your piece of string around something, perhaps the handle of a chest of drawers, a lamp on your bedside table, or an ornament of significance.

2   Feel into the energy of luck and imagine feelings of being delighted by luck and synchronicities. Close your eyes to help you focus. Hold that emotion while clasping the loose end of the string.

3   Tie a knot at the top of the piece of string, furthest away from you.

4   The next night, again, feel into the emotion and energy of being lucky and tie your second knot, about 1 cm (1/4 in) along from the last knot. Each time the knot is a little closer to you, and this symbolises drawing the energy of luck towards you.

5   Repeat this – one knot per night – for the remainder of January.

6   On the last day of the month, untie the string from its place, and tie the two ends together. You can keep it to use in meditation, as you might rosary beads; to aid concentration; and even wear it as a symbol of good luck around your wrist.

Raise your vibration

Mindfulness and manifesting can go hand in hand, even if at first they seem paradoxical – mindfulness encourages us to focus on the present moment and manifesting involves future desires.

So, how do we use mindfulness and manifesting to bring more luck into our lives? Practise this mindfulness meditation every morning before your day begins. Anchor fully into the present moment, to find your calm, to be open and receptive, and from that place take conscious, considered steps towards your dreams.

In order to manifest our desires, our nervous system needs to be regulated, our heart rate coherent and our mind open, aware and at ease. We cannot manifest when in a state of anxiety. Manifesting when we feel like this will only repel what we desire. So, you need to be able to comfortably anchor fully into the present moment and to regulate the mind–body connection. This can take some practice, so be patient with yourself. Setting an intention for mindfulness is a solid foundation on which all of your manifesting practices will build throughout the year.

NEW YEAR MEDITATION

Find a comfortable place to sit – a chair, bed or the floor. Become aware of your connection to where you sit. Notice, without changing anything, how you are holding your body. Notice how comfortable you are.

Take a big, deep breath, filling your lungs completely, before slowly releasing the breath, and relaxing the body.

Take another deep breath and start to notice how you feel in this moment, and what emotions are present for you right now. Notice how it feels to simply be you – right here, right now.

Take another deep breath and start to expand your awareness to notice any sounds around you. Take all your awareness to your ears before taking another deep inhale, and slowly exhale.

Now, take a moment or two to look up from this book and really notice the detail of the surroundings and environment you find yourself in. Bring your full awareness and focus into the present moment by engaging your senses. Feel the comfort found in this moment, free from the past.

For a moment, allow yourself to imagine all the luck, love and happiness yet to come in this new year ahead. Imagine all the experiences you are yet to experience. Feel a fizz of excitement in your heart and your belly, and allow the corners of your mouth to curl up into a smile.

Silently affirm to yourself: I believe in magic. I am naturally lucky. I am right where I am meant to be. Keep that smile on your face and take another delicious deep breath.

((CO

CHOOSE A SYMBOL
FOR THIS MONTH

Choose a photograph, drawing or sketch of a
symbol that resonates with you, to represent luck.
You might like to find your own or choose one
listed below. Display this symbol somewhere visual:
on your dresser, with your affirmations for this
month, on a designated pinboard or somewhere
you will come across it often, such as in your wallet,
on the back of your smartphone or in your glasses
case, for example. Every time you see the symbol,
let it be a reminder of your intention to feel lucky
and to recognise opportunities for luck this month.

CROSSED FINGERS

'Crossed fingers' is a pagan tradition for good luck. A cross was considered a symbol of good luck, as the intersection marked the joining of good spirits that would hold the energy of the wish until it came true. If a cross wasn't to hand when a wish was being made, two people would cross their index fingers over each other as a mark of good luck. Today, conveniently, it has become a solo, one-handed practice, crossing an index finger with the middle finger for good luck.

HORSESHOES

According to pagan folklore, horseshoes hung upright in a home act as a storage container for luck and good fortune, while also keeping bad spirits at bay. Horseshoes are made of iron, which is considered to possess magical powers that protect against evil spirits, while each horseshoe also contains seven holes, a lucky number for some.

ELEPHANTS

Elephants are a symbol of wisdom, protection and good luck in many cultures. In Hinduism, Ganesh, an elephant-headed god, was considered the remover of obstacles and is a symbol of luck and good fortune. In China, elephants are used in the practice of feng shui to bring about good luck within a home.

VELDISMAGN

This is an Icelandic rune (a symbol with cosmological power) that is used to protect against evil spirits and to bring good luck and good health.

The power of rituals

Pre-performance rituals are often performed by sportspeople before a race, a game or a match for good luck. English rugby player Jonny Wilkinson is famous for his iconic kicking ritual – clasping his hands together, judging the line of the ball to the post, with his bottom stuck out in a squat, before a penalty kick.

A good luck ritual such as this might be a superstitious act to increase a sense of confidence, but it is also performed to change the energy and vibration of the practitioner. In this case, the ritual is performed to quiet the mind and to align body-mind composure, even under immense pressure.

In an interview, Jonny Wilkinson explained: 'I've learnt how to centre my energy, relax and focus all the power I've got in my body into my legs so it's all there for the kick.' He would visualise the ball as if it were attached to a wire, and through centring his energy via his kicking ritual, he was able to activate muscle memory, achieve mental relaxation and engage a visualisation technique so that he could send the ball up the 'wire', bringing about his desire. Over time, a repeated ritual, such as this, helps the practitioner embody a vibration of luck and success.

Rituals like this that are performed to raise our vibration can be executed daily and can work for just about any situation; preparing for a big presentation or a job interview, before going on a first date, or simply starting each and every day with a raised vibration.

Your ritual might not look like Jonny Wilkinson's kicking ritual (and probably shouldn't!) but you're invited to play with the idea of visualising success this month. Visualise yourself running your first event, hitting a hole-in-one, or going on that first date, and step into the vision of you being the luck and success you desire. A very simple and popular visualisation practice for luck is to visualise a parking space when you need one!

A talisman for good luck

A talisman is an object that is said to hold magical powers. It might be an object worn, held or displayed somewhere of significance, to bring good fortune and luck.

Starting the new year with the intention to notice synchronicities and adopt an optimistic mindset can sometimes be the easy bit. Remembering to embody that intention can often be where people get stuck. Setting yourself up with little reminders of your intention, such as an intention-infused talisman that you will come across often, can help embed new habits and beliefs. Here is how to make your own talisman.

You will need

A coin (a pound, euro or dollar is fine)
Patchouli essential oil

1. To create your talisman, place the coin in direct sunlight and let it warm up. When the coin is warm, rub about three drops of patchouli oil into the coin and hold it between your hands as if in a prayer.

2. Feel the emotion and energy of good luck as you hold the coin. Whisper words of luck and gratitude, such as 'thank you for all the magic I receive'

or 'I attract luck and synchronicities into my year' into the coin. Set an intention for luck, and to feel lucky. Take your time to do this – truly feeling into the emotion of your intention is the most important aspect.

3. Close your intention setting practice by taking a few deep breaths.

4. Keep the coin in your pocket, or somewhere safe, as a talisman to attract good luck this month and to remind you of your intention to feel and be lucky.

5. At the end of the month, share the luck by gifting your coin to someone you know, or, you could leave your coin talisman somewhere for someone else to find.

The butterfly effect and luck

The butterfly effect, a principle of chaos theory, suggests that even the smallest, seemingly insignificant changes, choices and events can have a significant impact. Edward Lorenz, an MIT meteorology professor in the 1960s, came up with the idea while researching weather patterns. He linked the gentle flap of the wings of a butterfly on one side of the world to have the potential to change weather patterns thousands of miles away. Although he never claimed a direct link between one specific butterfly and a storm, the potential of something so small and insignificant having dramatic outcomes was indisputable through his mathematical and scientific reasoning.

So, the butterfly effect reminds us that the choices we make today have consequences and, ultimately, are what shape our future. It does also suggest that predicting the future is somewhat impossible. In order to manifest more of what we want in our lives, we need to make decisions aligned to that vision, today.

One of my favourite movies in the 1990s was *Sliding Doors*, starring Gwyneth Paltrow. In the opening scenes, we see the main character, played by Paltrow, miss her train. The film then follows two storylines: the events that follow if she misses the train, and what happens if she gets on the train. As a result of this one small, seemingly insignificant, everyday event, we watch how her entire destiny is altered.

Missing a train one morning in a rush to work might be defined in the moment as bad luck, but what if we were privy to the whole plot of our own destiny? Perhaps an inconvenient event is, in fact, a stroke of luck in disguise. I've often found myself identifying moments and events in my life as 'sliding doors moments', retrospectively seeing how one small choice, decision or event I had made changed the course of my own destiny.

Spend some time reflecting on your own 'sliding doors moments' throughout your life and identify any strokes of luck. I remember being absolutely gutted when I didn't get a job I really wanted in my early twenties, and it felt like the end of the world. Then, one month later, I was offered a job with a different company, which turned out to be one of the most unique and enjoyable working experiences of my life, one I would never have experienced if I had got the original job I had thought was meant for me. Not getting that job was a stroke of luck because the universe had a better plan for me. And so, when the inevitable inconvenience happens this month, and throughout the year, such as a long post-office line or a full café, see if you can adopt an attitude of gratitude and remember the butterfly effect – perhaps you are being looked after by a greater force, guiding you to a path that leads to more love, luck and magic than you could possibly imagine.

January's practice

This month we are playing with luck. In order to start embedding new beliefs about luck, you are going to start your morning with some positive affirmations, followed by a short, simple meditation to help you feel grounded and present. In the evening you are going to practise gratitude, which is one the most simple, yet essential, practices in manifesting anything you want.

Creating space in your day for a meditation practice can be challenging when you lead a busy life with lots of demands and distractions. If you are new to meditation, begin with 2 minutes and, over the course of the month, build up to 5 minutes.

Morning

Wake up and go to a mirror. Spend 30 seconds saying the affirmations on page 18 to yourself in the mirror. To help create the habit, you might choose to do this before or after brushing your teeth.

Next, find somewhere safe and comfortable to sit, and practise the mindfulness meditation on page 21. Set a timer for 2-5 minutes and welcome luck into your day. Do sit for longer if you are able to, or are already experienced with meditation.

Evening

Keep a gratitude journal to bring greater awareness of the luck you are manifesting. Put your journal at the side of your bed and, just before you turn the light out to drift off to sleep, jot down every coincidence and synchronicity, no matter how small. Add anything good and lucky you might have experienced that day, and anything that you're grateful for.

02

LOVE

FEBRUARY

'MANIFESTING ANYTHING INVOLVES
SELF-AWARENESS, ESPECIALLY
MANIFESTING LOVE'

ove is pure magic! We think of love as an emotion, but in its essence, it is energy. Experiencing love in any form can evoke feelings of safety and belonging, while romantic love can leave you feeling intoxicated and in love with life itself. In a spiritual sense, love is the foundation from which unity, compassion and all other spiritual attributes arise. Why would we not want to have more of *that* in our lives? Whether you are seeking to attract a new partner, deepen an existing romantic relationship or strengthen a sense of connection with family, pets or friends, manifesting love comes down to one thing – the relationship you have with yourself.

As we move into February, Imbolc marks the halfway point between the winter solstice and the spring equinox in the northern hemisphere, while Lammas, a celebration of harvest, is honoured in the southern hemisphere. Imbolc, sometimes referred to as Candlemas, is associated with the honouring of the Celtic goddess Brigit, goddess of wisdom, healing, protection and divine motherly love. Valentine's Day, which falls on 14 February, is a popular commercialised celebration recognised across the globe.

LIGHT A CANDLE

To honour love, light and connection this month, light three candles – one for self-love, one for the love you are manifesting, and one for love for the Earth and all beings.

Manifesting love

Practices for manifesting love are not concerned with manipulation techniques, game-playing or casting spells to influence or change other people. They involve raising the vibration of every cell of your being with radiant, magnetic, unalterable love, exactly as and where you are – and boy do they feel good to practise!

Manifesting anything involves self-awareness, especially manifesting love. The more you become aware of your own energy, and strengthen a loving relationship with yourself, the more love you will be able to manifest. The practices this month are about loving, trusting and staying true to yourself, whether you're single, married or anywhere in between. From a solid foundation of self-connection, you will feel more confident, be more open to receive, more able to ask for what you need and to set boundaries, and more willing to say yes to new experiences or push yourself out of your comfort zone in order to experience the love you desire. Love, just like magic, is energy, and energy requires space to flow and be expressed. If you want to change how much love you are experiencing, action of some kind is required.

It can be comforting to remember that everything that you desire already exists – how exciting is that? The love you are manifesting is also manifesting *you* – energetically and physically. For example, if you want a new romantic partner in your life, that person exists somewhere right now, dreaming of you. So then all you need to do is allow yourself to want what you want, prepare – by creating space – and most importantly, feel good as you are, where you are. When you are being unapologetically yourself, feeling whole and complete, you attract more of anything into life, including love. I hope you know you are worthy of the love you desire. Taking a leap of faith to open yourself up to receive love from a place of alignment will undoubtedly be worth it.

GET TO KNOW YOURSELF

Humans are wired for connection. Romantic relationships are often seen as one the greatest spiritual teachers, and for very good reason. Getting emotionally close and intimate with another requires you to allow yourself to be truly seen, flaws and all. It is a leap of faith into an unknown world of possibilities. For some, being without a relationship feels terrifying, while for others, letting someone in is their greatest fear. Relationships often reflect, expose and trigger the unhealed parts of ourselves, which is why it is so common for people to find themselves repeating unwanted patterns. There is a lot at play – and a lot to unpick – when you find yourself in a cycle such as this, partnered or otherwise. Understanding your attachment style, healing your inner child, and having a greater understanding of your core, often unconscious, beliefs about love, are all essential to initiate real change. This work can often take time, so tend to your heart gently and find support if you need to. You can't rush your healing.

Spend some time understanding your own beliefs (and blocks), by journaling the following reflection points throughout this month:

✧ What type of love would you like to manifest, and what is it specifically you would like to experience?

✧ What changes (mindset, physical, emotional . . .) do *you* need to make to accommodate more love?

✧ What are your deeper beliefs about love? Is love safe, scary, unstable? Do you feel worthy of love?

✧ What healing does your inner child need? What do they need to know about love? What do they need to hear?

✧ What is your relationship with yourself – do you love and accept yourself exactly as you are?

✧ What would the love you are manifesting feel like? How would it feel in your body?

✧ How would your life change experiencing this type of love? If you knew it was coming in the next seven days, what would you do to prepare?

A STORY OF TRUE LOVE

Hannah was approaching 37 and had been single for some time. Although she was living a happy life and was empowered and confident on her own, she decided it was time to call in her soulmate. She set up a ritual, lit a candle and started to write a list. She wanted to meet someone who was into similar sorts of things as her and she wanted to meet someone who shared some mutual friends. As her list of wants grew, she allowed her vision to come through stronger and be more specific. She added: someone who has an interest in photography, has lived in London before, has travelled a lot, has family in the county she was living in, and who wanted to have children. She got such a strong sense of who he was and what he was like, she could feel him as if he was already present in her life. She luxuriated in her visualisation before handing it over to the universe. She consciously said, and truly meant it, that she would be happy to wait for him to arrive . . . and then went about her day. Just three weeks later, she met her now husband and the father of their beautiful daughter.

Hannah believes in the power of the subconscious mind, claiming that if you are able to envision something with your conscious mind, and truly feel it and believe it on a cellular level, your subconscious and the universe work together to make it happen. Now, surrounded by the loves of her life – her husband and daughter – she would tell you that a simple manifesting practice can bring powerful, magical experiences. Hannah truly believes that you can manifest anything you want in your life, especially love.

Change your mindset

I want to share with you my own experience about mindset. A few years ago I caught myself, mid-thought, longing for a romantic companion. In a moment of mindfulness I realised there was an energy of 'longing' coursing through my body, heart and mind that also carried the energy of lack and self-victimisation. I didn't have what I wanted and it felt unfair. In awareness, I decided to switch my mindset. Instead of wallowing in longing, I flipped it in my mind, and chose to feel it as a delicious desire. I remembered that wanting a relationship isn't something tragic and sad, it is very human, and something positive and exciting to look forward to! My energy instantly changed in that moment. I felt energised, just by flipping my mindset from lack to desire. Which state do you think would be more magnetic for love?

This very subtle difference in mindset helped me completely shift the energy attached to one of my desires. It's like two sides of the same coin because the intention is the same – to be in a loving relationship – but one mindset projects a needy energy of scarcity and lack, while the other represents an excited, attractive sense of positive expectation. One feels heavy and lethargic, the other feels expectant and energising. Although this practice feels incredibly powerful when experienced, it isn't suggesting that you *pretend* you feel different to the way you do, or that you should feel guilty for feeling negative. It's more about flipping the way you feel in the moment from negative to positive, if you can and it feels good. All feelings are valid, because each and every one just shows us what matters to us. Simply becoming aware of your thoughts and feelings is the first step, then, with practice, flipping your mindset to be more positive will not only help you feel good in the moment but also more optimistic about the future. So, why not give it a try, with self-compassion?

Focus on how you feel in any given moment and you'll find a clue to the thoughts you are currently thinking and believing about yourself or your situation. Do you believe yourself to be someone worthy of love? Do you believe that love is good and safe? Are you desiring and magnetising love, or longing and grasping for it?

AFFIRMATIONS FOR LOVE

Repeat the following affirmations out loud to yourself in the mirror each morning to help reprogramme your subconscious mind to know the love that you already are:

- ✧ I am love
- ✧ I am worthy of love
- ✧ I am grateful for the love I already receive, and the love I am about to receive
- ✧ I love and accept myself, exactly as I am
- ✧ I am open and ready to give and receive love
- ✧ It is safe to love and be loved?

A SPELL FOR LOVE

Perform this spell on a Friday, during the waxing moon phase just after a full moon, preferably in the early morning. You will need about half an hour of uninterrupted quiet time. You can return and redo this spell throughout the month, if you choose, until the candles have burned out.

You will need

Smudging stick
A small sheet of baking paper
2 small pink or red taper/spell candles (with stands)
3 drops patchouli essential oil
3 drops frangipani essential oil
3 drops dragon's blood essential oil blend
1 tsp sugar
1 small handful of rose petals
2 rose quartz crystals (any size)
Matches

1. Smudge yourself (see page 7) before you begin. Lay the sheet of baking paper on a flat surface. Place the candles flat on the paper. Sprinkle the essential oils and sugar (holding back a pinch) over the candles and gently roll them around, covering the candles in the mixture. Sprinkle half the rose petals over the candles.

2. Place the candles into their stands close to each other, and place the crystals alongside. Sprinkle the remaining rose petals around the candles. Sprinkle the rest of the sugar around them.

3. Sit on the floor or a chair near your candles, and centre yourself with a few deep breaths. Set the intention to be present and focused for the duration of the practice. Close your eyes while you do this.

The more you are able to focus and not get distracted, the more intensity will go into the spell.

4. When you feel ready, light each candle, with one representing you, and one representing the love you wish to manifest (known or unknown). Summon up the feelings of love. Although recalling past feelings might be tempting, try not to attach the feeling of love to a specific person or experience – instead, focus on the energy of being in love. Try and imagine you are remembering the future, not the past. Sit there in complete love. Close your eyes while you do this.

5. You might find that your body responds positively to the feelings and emotion of pure love with a smile or a feeling of energy coursing through

you. Hold this feeling of love for the duration of your meditation. If you get distracted, it doesn't matter. Just let go of the distraction and return to the warm, fizzy, safe feeling of true love. Sit in meditation for as long as you can and feel comfortable. The spell will be completed, and cast, once the candles have burned out naturally on their own. If you need to stop the meditation before the candles have burned out, don't worry! Stub the candles out (make sure not to blow them out as this will cancel the spell).

Raising your vibration

In a metaphysical sense, love is the highest form of energy and it is pure essence, which is why you often hear people using 'love' as a secular alternative to god. Love is ever-present, all-encompassing and can never be destroyed. In a human sense, love is experienced from the inside out – it is yours to allow, give, receive and express whenever you choose. Your effort shouldn't be placed on trying to find it outside of yourself, but instead to embody it, exactly as you are.

According to the practice of tantra, sexual energy is the energy required to manifest *anything* we want, not just romantic love. Tantra is about sensuality and directing sexual energy in a joyful, balanced and healthy way to raise your energetic vibration and become more magnetic. Sexual energy is creative energy, and using it as fuel in any manifestation practice will undoubtedly increase the intensity given to it. When there is a healthy, unobstructed flow of sexual energy moving through the body, you feel more vibrant, attractive and confident. Sensuality basically means the engagement of our senses: sight, sound, taste, touch and smell, and through a deliberate practice of reconnecting to those senses, we open the flow. Tantra theory suggests that the earth and the body are the manifestation of divine energy, and that sexual energy is tasting divine energy, therefore both earth and body should be seen as sacred.

Tantra isn't just about sexual pleasure; it is about

celebrating the body and savouring sensuality. It is self-care in disguise! The body is our home, and so prioritising practices which help us feel good in our body will allow more energy to flow through. Integrating and embodying sensual, sexual energy in your body undoubtedly raises your vibration, and from a state of feeling good you are more easily able to manifest your desires. The next practice has its foundations in tantra.

A SACRED DANCE PRACTICE

Dance is a powerful way to help shift stuck energy in the body and to allow emotions to be expressed, which helps to raise your vibration. Find a song, or a playlist, that you really enjoy and makes you feel good.

Stand with both feet solidly rooted on the floor and feel the steadiness of your still body. Place both hands over your heart. Take a few deep breaths. Shake the hands out and allow the shake to move through your whole body, jumping up and down a little, releasing any tension in the body to the earth. You might like to make audible sounds as you release the energy from the body. Close your eyes while you do this.

Find stillness again, and raise your arms slowly up above your head, and imagine a warm, sensual nectar pouring down over your head and hands. Using your hands, play with the energy. As you imagine the nectar pouring down, roll your head and move your arms in an intuitive way that feels good.

Imagine the nectar slowly moving down through your whole body and allow this intuitive movement of flow, right down to the tips of your toes. Keep moving your body in any way that feels enjoyable. Notice how subtle, these movements feel, and allow any tension or emotions to be released. Allow your body to dance and move for as long as you like.

When you feel ready to stop, find a stable standing position once more, with your feet rooted on the floor. Place your hands back over your heart and take a few deep breaths. Smile before opening your eyes.

☾ ☾ ☾ ○

CHOOSE A SYMBOL
FOR THIS MONTH

Choose an image, drawing or sketch of a symbol
that resonates with you, to represent love. You
might like to find your own or choose one listed
below. Display this symbol somewhere you can
see it each day.
Let it be a reminder of your intention to manifest
love this month.

INFINITY SYMBOL

This looping figure of eight was invented by John Wallis, an English mathematician, in 1655, as a symbol to represent infinity. We can use it to represent an everlasting bond between two lovers.

MAPLE LEAF

Thanks to the abundant sweet sap of the maple tree, the maple leaf is a symbol of love, sweetness, generosity and awe, in Japan and China especially. The maple tree itself is a strong, stable tree able to withstand different conditions, so it also represents strong, everlasting love.

AGAPE

The rune agape represents unconditional love. Runes are symbols from an ancient Germanic alphabet (with Celtic and Norse variations) used for communication, magic and protection.

TWO SWANS

A pair of swans are a popular symbol for love because of the loyal, lifelong bond two swans form. They symbolise soulmates and true love. Aphrodite, the Greek goddess of beauty and sexual energy, was often depicted with a swan.

Visualise your future

I remember a coaching client once said to me that she wouldn't allow herself to visualise her desires because it made her feel sad that she didn't have them in that moment. What she didn't realise was that, by doing this, she was keeping herself in a cycle of lack. Allowing yourself to truly want what you want, lifting the lid on your desires, and to visualise them, is like lighting a beacon for your soul to be guided towards. Claiming your desires gives a clear message to the universe about what you want to receive, and that intention draws the present moment and the future dream closer together. Be clear on what love you want – light the beacon – then return fully to the present moment with gratitude; it's coming!

Grab a notepad and a pen. Allow yourself to really dream up, almost like daydreaming, the love you wish to manifest, as if you're watching the scene in a movie. Close your eyes if you like. Perhaps you imagine waking up in crisp white sheets with your lover next to you – how do the sheets feel, what do they smell like, how do you feel in your body while cuddling your lover? What is your lover like? How does your lover look at you? How do they interact with you?

Or perhaps you visualise yourself sat around a big dining table, just about to enjoy a feast with the love you wish to manifest. What food are you about to enjoy? What sounds are filling the room? Who is there?

Stay in this daydreamy state and start to write the scene in as much detail as you possibly can. Write it in the present tense and feel it as you write, so perhaps you let out a comforting, relaxed little sigh because of the cuddle you're receiving or your taste buds start to salivate at the smell of the dinner. When you are finished writing out this scene, let go of the visualisation, surrender it to the universe, and anchor yourself fully back into the present moment (no doubt feeling yummy!).

Returning to the present moment and working on feeling great, right here and now, as you are, is *essential* to this practice. Let go of *how* and *when* this dream will manifest and instead, simply choose to follow your bliss in the here and now, work on loving yourself and let the rest unfold in its own good time.

A MEDITATION ON LOVE

Prayers and poetry are the language of the soul. Reflecting on poetic verses, reading spiritual scriptures and speaking spiritual verses out loud are forms of meditation and are powerful tools for manifestation. Reflect on this poem about love, and notice how you feel. Return to it throughout the month if it resonates with you.

I was searching for love
in all the wrong places
in a person
a place or a role
mistaking that
once found
I grasp hold to make 'mine'
effort to hold the impermanent
as permanent
believing
there is something to lose

I realise now
love is right here

in the well of light
within my chest
always there
always accessible
nothing then to seek
but instead to notice
what I'm already a part of
finding peace
in remembering
there is nothing to lose

A talisman for love

Rose quartz is a popular talisman, believed to attract love and promote feelings for self-love. Rose quartz has an ancient lineage: beads made of rose quartz, dating back to 7000 **BC**, were found in Iraq and ancient Egyptians and Greeks were known to wear rose quartz jewellery for healing and protection. In Greek mythology rose quartz was also associated with Eros (a.k.a. Cupid), the god of desire and love, and Aphrodite, the goddess of desire.

You will need

A rose quartz

1. Carry a rose quartz in your pocket or your bra this month, or perhaps sleep with a rose quartz under your pillow to aid your manifestation practice.

Creating space for new love

Having a good spring clean and clear-out always feels good – just ask Marie Kondo! She suggests we declutter our houses and closets by asking ourselves, does each item 'spark joy'? What if we took the same approach to other areas of our life – thoughts, places, people and relationships?

Energetically letting go of the past, be that a past lover or even the disagreement you had yesterday with your current partner, will create space for new. Allowing yourself to deliberately and consciously fill the space created in your life with what you truly desire *is* the practice of manifestation.

Vacuum theory suggests that nature always seeks to fill gaps and holes – empty space cannot exist because nature is always trying to fill it with something new. Therefore, when you consciously let go of the old, you create space for the new. Life will keep filling the space created with old patterns and experiences, or you can start to consciously fill it with the new of your choosing. New thoughts, new energy, new desires, new behaviours, new versions of love – you choose.

Spend some time reflecting on creating new space during the month, through journaling or in conversation with a trusted friend. What thoughts, beliefs, people and experiences are you ready to let go of? Here are some ideas:

✧ Can you let go of focusing on the outcome or seeking control?

✧ Can you let go of unnecessary self-protection or your belief that you are not worthy of love?

✧ Can you let go of needing another person for you to feel validated, whole, worthy or complete?

✧ Can you let go of the lover you once were to create space for a new version of you to emerge?

February's practice

This month we are focusing on love. Each morning you are going to do some mood-boosting practices, to help you notice the many pleasures in life.

Morning

Just before your morning shower, play a song that feels good to you and move your body in any way that feels freeing and expressive. You can use the guidance found on page 43, or just intuitively move, dance and stretch your body.

As you are brushing your teeth, look at yourself in the mirror and give yourself a compliment. Remind yourself you are worthy, or repeat the affirmations found on page 39.

You are also invited to bring mindfulness and sensuality into your morning routine (don't worry, it doesn't need lots of time). For example, brush your hair with love and tenderness; feel the sensual nature of each morning shower; and practise mindful eating when enjoying your breakfast (eat slower and savour every bite). You don't need to do anything too different, just remember to savour and delight in the everyday pleasures.

03

PURPOSE

MARCH

'PURPOSE ISN'T SOMETHING YOU FIND,
IT IS SOMETHING YOU EMBODY'

ach of us has an inner calling, something that tugs at our curiosity and attention, and makes us feel in flow when we are doing it. This month we are going to explore purpose – the essence of *you*, something that comes naturally to you and that you would do whether you got paid or recognition for it, or not.

Purpose isn't something you find – it is something you embody. It is waiting within to be recognised and allowed, not obtained from outside of yourself. Adventures, experiences, people, conversations, triumphs and failures are all part of life's mystical aids that help you uncover your purpose, but ultimately, it is already yours to become.

The pagan celebration of Ostara, the goddess of spring, is honoured every March on the spring equinox in the northern hemisphere. It signifies the importance of planting seeds of intention for what you wish to blossom and bloom when the next season comes around. Manifesting purpose also requires just that: to plant seeds of intention and then to feed them and give them space and time to grow.

Held within a tiny acorn is the potential of a whole oak tree. In the very same way, your potential is housed within you to blossom and bloom into the person you are meant to be. Many of us are conditioned to label everything and organise things in boxes and people often mistake their purpose for a job title or role. The essence of purpose that you will be manifesting this month cannot be boxed or confined in this way. It is a truth you will embody and a contribution you will make, as you co-create a positive impact with the universe.

Listening to intuition

Perhaps you already know or have experienced that unnameable sense of calling that tugs on your soul and attention. Have you ever wondered what it is and where it comes from? It is that tug of intuition that you must surrender to in order to embody your purpose. That pull of intuition is understood by diving deep into the nature of consciousness and the energy of the universe that is not 'personal'. It is not the things that I call me – my name, my personality, my age or gender. It is a universal energy that connects us all – call it collective consciousness, universe, spirit, creative energy or god. Your purpose is your unique gift shared with the world.

In Hindu and Buddhist philosophies, purpose is referred to as dharma, a divine law that implies you are duty-bound to fulfil during your time here on this planet. I kind of like the idea of making that promise, to evolve to become the truest expression of myself over my lifetime, to be of benefit to the world. Are you up for making the same commitment?

Manifesting purpose is about becoming more of who you truly are, allowing creative energy to guide you to live out your true potential. Your purpose is to be authentically *you*, and live your life in some form of service to the world. Some people contribute through their art, their compassion for animals, their respect for plants, their drive to improve the well-being or welfare of others, to heal, entertain or to uplift. Your purpose is already expressing itself through you, in the things you do naturally or the actions you take unconsciously – you simply need to pay attention to notice it.

GET TO KNOW YOURSELF

Are you ready to think about what your purpose
might be? Spend some time in quiet reflection
and journal your answers to the following
prompts. Allow your answers to pour onto the
page as a stream of consciousness, unedited and
answered quickly, without judgement.

✧ What comes easily to you?

✧ What do you spend most of your
time doing?

✧ If you knew you only had one
year left to live, how would you
spend your time and what would
you want to accomplish or
experience?

✧ What activities light you up?

✧ What did you enjoy doing as a
child? What make-believe games
did you play, what were your
favourite toys, what activities did
you enjoy the most? What books
did you read over and over?

✧ Who were your idols or role
models growing up and what
was it you loved about them?

✧ What gets you out of bed in the
morning? What would you be
excited to do?

A STORY OF DOING WHAT YOU LOVE

Beth Kempton, successful author and entrepreneur, has a motto: 'Life is too short to *not* do what you love.' She has positively impacted and inspired thousands of people around the world to live their lives on purpose. In order to manifest purpose in her own life, she admits she had to let go of logic and follow her intuition instead, redefine what success meant to her, and really tune in to let the quiet voice within guide her along a path that felt good and in flow. She claims this surrender, to life and to her intuition, has changed her life.

The bridge between intuition and purpose, she believes, is guided strongly by synchronicity. So much so that Beth claims that everything good that has happened in her own life can be traced back through synchronicities, from business partnerships to book deals.

For example, when she was writing her first book, *Freedom Seeker* (2017), which has a metaphor of a bird running through it, she started to notice that every time she doubted herself, a feather would appear. She remembers one morning, when feeling overwhelmed with self-doubt, she opened her front door to a lawn full of feathers. She made her way to a café to meet a friend and walked past a woman with a peacock feather tattooed across her scalp. Her friend arrived in a feather-print dress. The barista was wearing feather earrings and was trying to shoo a trapped bird out of the café, just as a truck drove past the window with a giant feather printed across the side! She saw every sign as a reminder of the essence of the book itself – taking flight and soaring from feeling trapped to living free, living a life filled with a sense of purpose. Beth believes you can read whatever you like into signs, but to her, they are unmissable guidance on a path to purpose, and proof that you are waking up.

Change your mind

Uncovering your purpose may require undoing the conditioning you've been programmed to believe about yourself, the world around you and how your life 'should' be. A friend of mine recently came out of 22 years' service in the military and, after 22 years of being told how to think, where to be and what to do, he found there was a whole new world waiting for him to explore, including who he was within it. It struck me that each of us have our own version of this, just with a different set of circumstances to his.

Our own upbringing and life experiences, including societal or family pressures that guide us toward conforming and away from our true nature, require an undoing. Embodying your purpose is about getting in touch with your authenticity and your intuition (you will explore manifesting intuition more on page 198). Living on purpose is a magical combination of embodying your passion and gifts, and sharing them in service of the world. It requires equal parts action and effortless surrender.

What I mean by surrender is allowing the flow of energy and life to move through you, trusting yourself and the universe as you go. When you are fully present in the moment, you are able to follow the breadcrumbs that appear on your path, via synchronicities and signs, inviting you to follow your bliss and sense of purpose. Ultimately, surrendering is to be who you truly are. It feels liberating to be in the presence of someone who is truly, unapologetically themselves. There are some shining examples of people in the public eye who are loving their craft, empowering others and shining as their authentic selves – Jonathan Van Ness, Alicia Keys, Luvvie Ajayi Jones, Laverne Cox and Sophia Bush spring to mind for me, and

I'm sure you can think of others. Follow your curiosity and your bliss, and embody your truth! What would it be like to be unapologetically 'you' and to shine bright just as you are?

AFFIRMATION FOR PURPOSE

The practice this month is to notice when you shrink yourself. You know those times when you don't speak up, or hide your talents or truth, perhaps so as to not offend or irritate others, or out of shyness? Notice, without judgement, when this happens, and practise self-soothing that part of you, with acknowledgement and appreciation for trying to keep you safe. Then place a hand on your heart and affirm:

✧ We don't need to do that anymore. I am safe to be and express who I truly am. It is safe to be me.

A sacred prayer

Connect to your purpose with this sacred prayer. This can be read silently or spoken out loud, as a conversation between you and the universe. Choose a word that you personally feel comfortable with to describe the force and energy much bigger than you. This prayer can be read each morning as part of your daily routine for March found on page 70, or simply when you feel the need to reconnect to your purpose and the energy that binds you with it.

Dear universe/guides/light/love/spirit/god/creativity,

Thank you for this day, an opportunity to live, love and create as your co-pilot. Remind me to choose my actions, my words, my thoughts consciously so to be the love and kindness that I seek. I invite you to live through me today.

Remind me of my compassionate essence and that I am love, even when I am in the darkness. I invite the life that wants to live through me? Support me to be the truest expression of myself so that I can light the way for others.

I invite the child in me to play, knowing they are safe, welcome, loved and worthy. Integrate my inner child with who I am in this moment, so that I can hear and trust their intuition, curiosity and joy, and follow it. I am the safe container and divine guardian for my inner child now. I invite the elder in me, the sage, the wise future self, to be present with me today; their guidance feels so comforting and reminds me I am home.

I am grateful to the flesh, blood and the bones of this human body, and for this thinking mind and willing heart – thank you. I invite magic, signs and synchronicities into this day to remind me of my purpose and mission here on Earth.

Remind me to be authentic, brave and trusting, and that, ultimately, I am here to learn and to play. I promise to yield to the flow of life that is carrying me today and every day. I promise to rest when I need to; to trust in the unfolding; to open when I feel the reflex to close; to believe in myself and my worth.

Thank you for this day, an opportunity to live, love and create as your co-pilot. Thank you, thank you, thank you.

Interpret the symbolism of your dreams

Dream interpretation was popularised by Carl Jung and Sigmund Freud in the 19th century, but it has been a potent aspect of ancient practices for millennia. Jung, among other psychologists, suggested that dreams are one way in which the subconscious mind communicates with us, while also acting as a way for the brain to process emotions and experiences. Just as it is with a manifesting practice, effectively interpreting dreams requires you to pay attention to the *feeling* you experienced, and the symbolism of the images you saw, rather than concerning yourself with, or becoming too attached to, the specific 'things' in the dream.

The feelings expressed within a dream, thanks to all its wild and wonderful plot twists and seemingly nonsensical expressions, reveal your innermost desires and fears. Jungian dream analysis also suggests that every aspect of your dream represents a part of you: the lover you encounter, the bear you are being chased by, the rollercoaster you are riding, are all representations of the different aspects of your psyche, thoughts and how you are interpreting your waking life. The subconscious mind is always absorbing, processing and storing information, much more than our conscious mind can conceive. An alignment of the subconscious and conscious mind is essential to manifestation, as our dreams provide us with vital information along our manifesting journey. Paying attention to your dreams will help you understand your deeper fears, thoughts, desires and beliefs. It might also provide you with creative ideas and precognitive information – otherwise known as premonitions.

Famously, Dmitri Mendeleev wrote the periodic table

after falling asleep and dreaming of a table where all the elements fell into place! Some of my most creative ideas and insights have come to me in my dreams, along with some of the most challenging insights and memories, which was all part of and essential to my healing and my manifesting journey.

KEEP A DREAM JOURNAL

This month you are going to keep a dream journal. The idea is that you try and record your dreams each night to build up a picture at the end of the month.

Before you go to sleep at night, prepare your journal and pen at the side of the bed, and set the intention to remember your dreams before you drift off to sleep.

As soon as you wake up, while still in the liminal state between sleep and wakefulness, record the content of your dreams, either by writing or drawing pictures. Note the main emotions you experienced and as much detail as you can remember. You don't need to give too much effort to analysing each dream individually now, as the analysis will come at the end of the month.

At the end of the month, look back at your dreams and notice if there are any patterns or recurring messages.

✧ Can you get a sense of what your subconscious mind is processing?

✧ What fears are present for you?

✧ What are your deeper desires?

✧ Are the things you are manifesting making their way into your dreams?

✧ Are the things you are dreaming about coming true in your waking reality?

My own purpose

I believe writing, and creating opportunities for people to reconnect with themselves, is my purpose. The journey I've been on in order for this book to be in your hands is one of perseverance, resilience, dedication, joy and magic. It was a dream I had and worked tirelessly towards. I took action by sharing my writing anywhere I could, visualising, practising rituals, having fun and being resilient to the many, many rejections I received along the way.

One ritual I performed was to really allow myself to dream, and to write it down. I remember being on a packed rush-hour London Tube, on my 45-minute commute home from work. As the train rattled along, I closed my eyes and I allowed myself to dream. I imagined living by the beach in Cornwall, working for myself, running well-being retreats and owning a little dog. I got my phone out of my bag and scrolled forward three years in my calendar and set an alarm on a note to myself called 'three years from now.' I listed all the contents of my daydream, and then forgot all about it.

Three years rolled by and an alarm went off on my phone. I couldn't believe it! I was living in Cornwall with my beloved dog and I was running retreats! I was so enthralled by the feeling, I did it again. I scrolled forward another three years, this time listing 'travel for work', 'run a retreat in Mexico' and 'have articles published in magazines'.

Three years later and I had spent a summer teaching meditation in Indonesia, travelled to Sri Lanka for work, had run a retreat in Mexico and was writing regularly for a number of well-being magazines. So I did it again, next time listing a published book! Not everything came to fruition within my notes, but there was progress towards each and every desire I listed – a stepping stone towards it. Progress is a mixture of intention, action, trust and surrender, along with many magical moments of synchronicity along the way.

SET YOUR INTENTION

Now it's your turn! Allow yourself to daydream of your life ahead, as if recalling a future memory. Then start to list the contents of your daydream in a note in your phone calendar, three years from now. Write it in the first person: 'I am working with animals', 'I am a parent' – whatever you think is your purpose. Set an alarm, so the note alerts you when the time comes around. Then forget all about it. Surrender it to the universe.

Acts of kindness

Think back to the idea of planting seeds of positive action that I mentioned at the start of the chapter. Acts of kindness and generosity raise your vibration because they evoke positive emotions and good feelings about yourself and the world. Consciously choosing to perform a random act of kindness or spontaneous generosity will always, without doubt, make you feel better. A study carried out by Sophie Ekrod in 2019 concluded that doing random acts of kindness significantly improves depressive symptoms and mental well-being. So performing a random act of kindness, like giving or sharing something, is a tangible thing you can do which will lift your spirits and raise your vibration. It won't solve all your problems, but it will feel good, and following what feels good will lead you to your purpose.

As I write this in 2022, there are several videos going viral from Instagram and YouTube accounts who solely exist to gift money to strangers as a random act of kindness. A friend's son, Fin, showed me one, where a presenter asked strangers for help – perhaps a dollar to make a phone call – and if they showed him kindness, he gifted them $500 or more. Science proves that not only do random acts of kindness feel good for the giver and receiver, but even observing them also makes the observer feel good. One act of kindness therefore ripples in all different directions, raising the vibration of feel-good energy around you.

So, the practice this month is to perform one random act of kindness each day in March. Do whatever comes naturally to you, and keep a note of what you did and how it made you feel. Here are some ideas to get you started:

- ✧ Write a note to a stranger and leave it on a park bench to brighten their day

- ✧ Buy a copy of your favourite book for a stranger – leave it somewhere or in the book shop to be given to someone of their choosing

- ✧ Paint a picture as a gift

- ✧ Knit a scarf, hat or baby booties

- ✧ Tip a waiter with extra generosity

Your vibration will be of service, kindness and generosity, and that energy will be matched by the universe; it is always so. Looking back over your random acts of kindness will help you to recognise if there was a pattern or theme to them, offering you an insight to your purpose.

A MEDITATION ON PURPOSE

Read this meditative poem whenever you need grounding into a sense of calm and purpose, or need reminding that you are already enough.

each fleeting feeling carries its own energetic charge
infusing itself in the atmosphere in your chest
and the messages sent by your heart, in ripples and waves

like a rip current surge beneath this ocean surface
you're pulled back and forth from your own centre
leading you far from the course you thought you had so
    carefully mapped
in your vessel of one you batten down hatches
and navigate a fickle sea of others and things
consumed by the drama, you forget your inner guidance and
    your own centre of calm
you change course with the wind, on a hunch or the call of a
    misplaced heartbeat meant for another time
you think you're separate from the purpose that you seek
that life should be lived in the space of efforting
that somehow it is your responsibility to convince the waves into
    taming, in order to find balance
yet at the depths of the ocean there is always calm
even when the waves are raging war against the skies
let the surrendered gap between each out breath, before the
    drawing in of new life, new energy, remind you of your own
    depths, your own inner guidance, your own sense of calm
breathe deeply and be reminded:
you are worthy, you are ready and you are already enough

A talisman for purpose

Selenite is a powerful crystal to help with mental decluttering. Often, when you feel like you are unable to hear your inner calling, it's because there is too much noise and thought chatter going on in your head.

You will need

A selenite stone

---

1. Sleep with the selenite tumblestone under your pillow this month to aid with mental clarity of thought during the day, and to help clear the path for intuition to flow through you at night.

Understand the path of least resistance

Although living your purpose requires action and effort, it doesn't mean swimming against the stream in a struggle – quite the opposite. When it comes to manifesting purpose, you will accomplish more by striving less. Do what comes easily to you and what lights you up. It is the difference between trying to force a square peg to fit into a round hole and finding the square hole for the peg you've got!

Manifesting your purpose does require you to have a clear intention and to take action, but it also requires you to remain spontaneous, allowing no resistance to the life that is carrying you and calling you. The natural world provides us with a perfect example of this: water always finds the path of least resistance in order to meet the ocean. Sometimes the course of your path isn't exactly how you thought it would be, or the twist and turns feel like you aren't making progress, but when you yield to the flow you are being carried in, you open yourself up to experiencing synchronicity.

Choosing the path of least resistance is to dismantle the 'shoulds' you might have placed on yourself in life (I should be . . ., this should be . . ., I should do . . ., they should do . . .) and instead live in a state of flow and harmony with what *is*. Instead of resisting the things you cannot change – people, certain circumstances, etc. – and desperately trying to control the outcome of your manifestation, practise accepting what is before you. Trust it is meant to be, take responsibility for what you choose next and do what feels right and good in that moment. Are you ready to let yourself be who you truly are?

March's practice

This month we are focusing on purpose.

Morning

Each morning, jot down your dreams from the night before (as instructed on page 63).

Any time when needed

At some point in the day, light a candle and spend 5 minutes in quiet meditation. Make a note of the below points in your journal and then read the poem found on page 61 out loud before blowing the candle out.

✧ Three things you are good at

✧ Three things you enjoy

✧ Three things that feel good to you

✧ Three things you will do for others (or the planet)

04

COMMUNITY

APRIL

'LIVING IN ALIGNMENT WITH OTHERS
AND CO-CREATING MAGIC CAN ALLOW
MORE SYNCHRONICITIES AND
OPPORTUNITIES TO UNFOLD'

There is a popular saying that suggests 'your vibe attracts your tribe'. Manifesting a community, and a sense of belonging for yourself, means consciously choosing the relationships and activities you invest your time and energy in. As your connections deepen, your vibration and sense of well-being increases and, to be honest, the world needs more of that right now.

Belonging to a community of people who understand you on a deeper level, who have similar values, aspirations and goals, and who enjoy similar activities is fuel to manifesting other areas of your life, too. Living in alignment with others and co-creating magic can allow more synchronicities and opportunities to unfold.

April is a thriving month in many religious calendars for festivals and community celebrations, including Ramadan, Passover and Easter. Buddhist new-year celebrations take place on the first full moon in April and although there are different traditions, it is commonly a celebration of renewal. Songkran is the new-year celebration in Thailand, and is a joyous community affair, where communities often take to the streets to participate in mass water-throwing. What fun! In the pagan calendar, April is associated with new life and fertility, and is the month of preparation for the future harvest in the northern hemisphere. It seems that April is a thriving month for community celebrations across the globe, and so we will make it our focus this month too!

When manifesting, we often have to look back in order to prepare for the future. Seeking to belong to a group of people outside of your family is hardwired into your genetic programming. My DNA ancestry can be traced back to the land I call home today, and I often reflect on what it would have been like for my ancestors of the Neolithic tribes of England, whose footsteps I walk in today. Their survival would have been reliant on social belonging, so it is no wonder that the desire to belong is so unshakable in most of us.

Social belonging isn't the only type of 'belonging' that tribes from all over the world, lost and surviving, experience. They also belong to the earth, live in harmony with the seasons, and honour the natural world as sacred. Their relationship with the land, and to each other, is something lost in modern Western culture. The sense of disconnection is so rife, in fact, that it has resulted in an epidemic of loneliness. Among many other things, ancient and surviving tribes from all over the world teach us of the importance of community, ceremony, rites of passage, rituals and honouring sacred sites. When you bond as people, and to the earth, you bind together in a different frequency.

Being in a group of people is different to feeling as if you belong there. According to a study carried out by Alyson Mahar, Virginie Cobigo and Heather Stuart in 2012, belonging is a subjective feeling of value and respect derived from a reciprocal relationship. It is built on a foundation of shared experiences, beliefs or personal characteristics. It is being in a group which one chooses, wants and feels permission belonging in. In order to attract a like-minded community, you must be your true self so they can find you.

FINDING YOUR PEOPLE

In order to belong to a group, you must put yourself out there and join in. In order to have good friends, you must be a good friend yourself. In order to feel a sense of connection and belonging to the earth, you must consciously remember your place within it and reconnect. In order to spend time with people who really inspire you, you must embody the inspiration you desire. Manifesting your community is about becoming the friend, neighbour and stranger you want to meet, and it is about participating. Spend some time journaling these questions this month:

✧ Who do you feel most connected to, and why?

✧ What makes a good friend? What attributes do you admire?

✧ In an ideal world, what activities would you like to do with your community or group of friends? What would bring you together?

✧ What community values are most important to you?

✧ What do you want to talk about with your community or group of friends?

✧ What beliefs or experiences might be holding you back from being part of a community you desire?

✧ Describe your connection to the natural world. What could you do to honour and deepen that connection?

A STORY OF MANIFESTING COMMUNITY

In 2014, professional dancer Illana Gambrill opened the doors to a small sports hall to lead her first weekly dance class for the public. Illana's intention was to bring the joy and power of dance to everyday people, not just professionals, and to bring the love of dance back for herself too. Her vision was humble to start with: it was simply to offer a space for local people to join in, be themselves, feel safe, unleash, feel confident and to dance together in a community. As the classes began to grow, Illana saw the life-changing impact they were having on people's lives. She realised the power of what she was creating – community – and she allowed her vision to expand. She visualised a long line of people queuing up at the front door and a studio packed full of people wanting to feel alive, be part of a community and to feel amazing within their own skin. She wrote down everything she saw in her mind and said it out loud.

The classes grew, and she remembers in 2018, when she returned from a short holiday, she was greeted by a long line of people queuing to get in and a studio filled to capacity with people from all walks of life – ready to dance, just as she imagined. Today, Illana leads a thriving keep-fit dance community of thousands of people all over the world. She radiates authenticity, empowerment and positivity and is the embodiment of someone living out her purpose and sharing her gifts with a community she very clearly loves.

Illana told me that she believes that the right mindset, visualisation and dreaming big are key to her manifesting practices. She also writes down her intentions and speaks them out loud to anyone, and wherever she can. Her hope for others is that they stop worrying about what to do or when things are going to happen, but instead, to simply place one foot in front of the other in the direction of what feels good, and to have absolute trust that whatever you are manifesting will come when the time is right.

Is anything holding you back?

Your community is out there and you are already welcome within it. Though perhaps there are a number of blocks that might be in the way of you and your soul community. A limiting view a lot of people hold, myself included, is a subconscious belief that you are not welcome. It is a belief that may have been formed in school, thanks to the phenomenon of the 'popular' kids, or through family dynamics. When you shrink and hide parts of yourself for fear of persecution or of not being welcome you are also limiting the possibilities of forming deeper relationships with people who are on your wavelength. Your own judgement of people, or fear of judgement *from* people, acts as a block. Lacking confidence to put yourself out there and try something new also creates resistance. One thing is for certain: you can't manifest a community without getting out there and being part of one.

Manifesting a community on a soul level requires you to let go of judgement, to open yourself up to others and to be yourself completely. It also requires you to accept others exactly as they are too. You are part of cyclical nature and will change and evolve throughout your lifetime. Some friendships grow in the same direction while others drift apart. Allowing this natural flow of connection, without resentment or blame, is a beautiful thing. Friendship is about reciprocity. As you change and transform, grant yourself permission to be supported, seen and held by friends walking the same path, and step out of your comfort zone to try something new.

AFFIRMATIONS FOR COMMUNITY

Repeat these simple affirmations throughout the month:

- ✧ I am welcome
- ✧ I am wanted
- ✧ I am safe
- ✧ I belong here
- ✧ I am home

A SPELL FOR SOUL FRIENDS

Having a trusted circle of friends, no matter the size, is a beautiful thing. Soul friends champion you on your journey towards your dreams and celebrate with you when you achieve them. They are right there when times get tough and you need a hand to hold.

Perform this spell on the new moon this month, during daylight hours, to call in your soul friends.

You will need

Pink candle
Pen and paper
Glue stick
An image that represents the friendship or
community you wish to belong to
1 tbsp dried passion flower
A piece of string, cord or wool
A small amethyst crystal

1. When you are settled, grounded and ready to begin, light the candle to signify the start of your ritual.

2. On the piece of paper, write a list of the activities you will do together with your new community. Imagine how you will feel when you are taking part in these activities, and infuse the feeling of belonging and safety into the paper.

3. Glue the image that represents your friendship circle next to your list. Next, write out a list of what you would bring to friendship circle, and how you will embody friendship qualities and attributes.

4. Rub some glue onto the paper. Say the following prayer as you scatter the dried passion flower onto the paper and glue: 'I call in my soul community. I welcome you in as you welcome me. We support, champion, lift and elevate each other. We are one.'

5. Roll the paper up into a scroll and tie the string around it before stubbing out the candle.

6. Place the scroll in a sunny spot in your house in direct sunlight, next to the amethyst crystal and leave it there for the month. Then take action to get out there: join a class, reach out and send the text, sign up to a new course, join a sports team.

7. After the month is up, place the scroll to one side. Perhaps you'll stumble across it in months or years to come and be pleasantly surprised!

(((◯

A SYMBOL FOR
THIS MONTH

You might wish to focus on manifesting a deeper connection with family, friend or the wider community this month. Pay attention and notice if the following symbols appear in your awareness, via dreams or synchronicities in your day-to-day life.

You may also wish to choose one of the following symbols that represents community most to you. You can sketch the symbol or purchase the physical item, or find an image and display it somewhere you will see it often, to remind you of your intention and to draw the energy of community closer to you.

CELTIC TRIANGLE (OR KNOT)

Rooted in paganism, the Celtic knot symbolises family, unity and protection. Many interwoven symbols and designs are common in the pagan traditions as the three points also represent the cyclical nature of all things: earth, air and water, or birth, life and death.

FRIENDSHIP BRACELETS

Friendship bracelets are a beautiful symbol for the sacred platonic bond between people. Knot tying, or macramé, which is the Arabic word for 'fringe', dates back to the 13th century, and macramé is considered to be the origin of the friendship bracelet. For Native American cultures, making a friendship bracelet must be done with the friend in mind, granting the recipient a wish, which will be braided into the bracelet on the last knot. In order for the wish to come true, the bracelet must fall off naturally, and then the wish will have been cast. Friendship bracelets can be found in a number of cultures in Central and South America, India and China, to name but a few.

PIKORUA (TWIST)

Pikorua is a Māori symbol that stands for partnership, friendship and an eternal bond. It is a double-twisted shape symbolising the twist of the pikopiko fern. It represents the eternal bond between the spirits of people or cultures across time and space. The separate twists symbolise individual paths, yet the interlacing represents an eternal bond, always returning to each other.

TWO ARROWS CROSSED

Two arrows crossing over each other symbolise paths crossing, a deep connection and friendship. Within Native American culture, crossed arrows represent allegiance.

WELL

A water well is a symbol of life, community and cooperation. A well represents the central point of a village and a natural resource shared by all equally. It also represents the human connection to the natural world, as we are unable to survive without water. On a spiritual level, the well can often symbolise collective consciousness, with the well being the drawing of life-force energy through the human experience.

Visualise this

In the dreamy, liminal state between wakefulness and drifting off to sleep at night, let yourself consciously dream. Spend some time this month visualising yourself being a good friend, sitting in a circle with soul friends, giving and receiving support and love from them, just before you drift off to sleep. Let this be a visualisation predominantly filled with the feeling of gratitude, for the friends you already have and for the friends you are calling in. No matter the community you are part of, or lack of one that you currently find yourself in, really feel the love during the visualisation. Indulge the daydream in whatever direction you feel called; a day out together, work collaborations, sister circles, travelling adventures – you decide.

Raise your vibration

Moving your body and getting your heart pumping is essential for physical and mental wellbeing – and for manifesting. When you exercise, 'feel-good' hormones are released, such as serotonin, endorphins and dopamine, which act as magical fuel to any manifesting practice. When you feel good, your vibration is higher and you are more easily able to manifest your desires. Movement of any kind helps shift stuck energy in the body and can even support creative thinking. I know my best ideas come to me when I go on a long walk. Regular exercise is a catalyst for energy too – the more you move your body in a healthy way, the more energy you have.

Community is part of this as well. Studies have shown that attending mass gatherings, such as festivals, increases an individual's sense of belonging to humanity and enhances a sense of coherence between mind, body and heart. Group movement, such as dancing, sports and exercise classes, also produces these effects. It is fun to think that half of the high you experience when you go to a gig to see your favourite musical artist is the coherence you're experiencing among the community of fans.

Your challenge this month is to seek out a group gathering, such as an exercise class or a concert to attend – something that would allow you to move your body and share your space with others with similar interests who are there to do the same. Before you attend, remind yourself of your intention to meet like-minded soul friends, and then let go and simply have some fun.

A MEDITATION FOR COMMUNITY

This month's meditation is about networks and the many ways you are connected to the world around you.

If you can take yourself to a forest or wood for this meditation, that would be great. Otherwise, you can simply imagine that you are there.

Sit directly on the ground, surrounded by trees (if possible). Take a few moments to settle yourself by closing your eyes, and taking a few long, slow, deep breaths. Feel the support of the earth beneath you.

Start by consciously connecting with each breath and become aware of the exchange between you and the trees. As you breathe in fresh air, the tree breathes out. As you breathe out, the tree breathes in. It is a constant life-giving cycle of exchange which happens all on its own, without your doing or even awareness. Feel into a sense of gratitude for this effortless exchange.

As you are sitting on the earth, imagine the networks of roots beneath the ground around you, an unseen world of intelligence and communication between the trees. Feel the web of connection between you and your friends, past, present and future, unseen yet bound with reciprocity and natural connection. Feel into a sense of gratitude for them all.

Take a deep breath and remember the sky and cosmos above the trees, almost taking a bird's-eye view of the Earth. See the web of connection between Earth and beings, communities and families, all as one ecosystem.

Take another deep breath and draw your awareness back into your own heart. Place one hand down onto the earth, and one hand over your heart. Bring a smile to your face and feel the connection and generosity of the earth, and set the intention to show the same to it.

When you are ready, open your eyes and enjoy a few moments sitting in stillness and notice the colours, shapes, textures and shades of the trees around you.

Join a community circle

Intentionally gathering in an intimate, trusted group to support each other, perform rituals, ceremonies and rites of passage, is evident throughout history and particularly in native cultures and in witchcraft. The resurgence of sister/women's circles, and men's circles, has begun to gain traction once again in the West.

A circle is held as a ceremony, providing a safe container for honest communication, personal intention-setting and the co-creating of magic. A circle usually involves meeting regularly, often monthly or even weekly, to focus on a specific intention. Activities may vary, but generally include meditation, ritual, prayers or spells of some kind. There is so much power in attending such events.

If there are no circles in your local area, you could find one online or instigate a circle yourself. Where exercise classes and mass group gatherings for entertainment can help improve your physical health, circle gatherings tend to your emotional health. All help raise your vibration, feel good and help you take action towards manifesting your soul friends.

Understand the law of action

The law of action is a universal law that says exactly what it is on the tin. In order for you to see change happen in your physical and personal reality, *you* must take action. When you take action that is aligned with your deepest desires, you manifest a new world for yourself and others – it is that simple.

When considering the ancient wisdom of our ancestors and indigenous tribes all over the world, we must take the law of action seriously – the survival of our human family on this Earth depends on it. What you are manifesting and the actions you take today, have an impact on future generations to come. For example, the vision and actions of each Suffragette transformed the world that I and other women in the UK get to live in today. The actions you take individually and with your community may change the course of history for your children, grandchildren and for the Earth. You must take action to enable change. If you want to be in a high-vibe community, with a deep soul connection, you must take action of some kind to find it, attract it and to be part of it.

What kind of world are you manifesting for your grandchildren? Are the actions you are taking in the greatest interest of generations to come? Is what you are manifesting for the greater good of others or just for yourself? Are you considering what you can bring to a community or friendship, as well as what you can take?

April's practice

Every day this month, take one conscious action that is of service to your community. It could be picking up a piece of litter; helping a neighbour; calling or texting a friend to check in on them; stopping to speak with a homeless person for a few minutes; putting a few coins in a charity collection pot; or joining a craft group or dance class, for example. Keep a note of each random act of kindness, service or connection in your journal. This might be in list form, or sketched or drawn. You can repeat the same actions often, but just ensure you take one small action each day and keep a note of it. Over the month, watch the web of connections and the community that you are part of become known to you across the page.

05

JOY

MAY

'YOU WILL ONLY FEEL MORE JOY IF
YOU ALLOW YOURSELF TO FEEL'

This month we are going to playfully launch ourselves into exploring joy, delight and exaltation. Joy is defined by the Merriam-Webster dictionary as: 'The emotion evoked by well-being, success or good fortune, or by the prospect of processing one's desires'. The prospect of processing one's desires is what we might otherwise recognise as manifesting!

Joy is the very essence of human nature, often embodied clearly by children and animals. Just before I sat down to write this chapter I took my jolly, joy-spreading little terrier for a walk. He, as many dogs do, evokes joy within strangers effortlessly, just by merrily trotting along or delighting in absolutely everything he comes across.

Joy is a creative, life-force energy often expressed through laughter, dancing and a childlike sense of curiosity and wonder. Experiencing joy, smiling and experiencing positive emotions has a number of health benefits and has even been linked to prolonged life.

Joy is found in the experiences that are happening right now, not out there in the future. Joy is the expression of rejoicing in your blessings, acknowledging the synchronicities, and strengthening your connection to the universe as you go along. Finding delight in the evolution of your desires is the essence of manifesting itself. Placing joy as the intention for your moment-to-moment experiences will shift your whole vibration and experience of living. Joy can be found in the simplest, most natural of things. Still, if at times you can't find joy, look for the source of it instead: delight.

May Day, also known as Beltane, is the halfway point between the spring and the summer solstice in the northern hemisphere, and it is celebrated as an official holiday in over 60 countries. 'Beltane' is a Celtic word meaning 'the fires of Bel', a Celtic goddess. Therefore, Beltane celebrations were referred to as the fire festival, welcoming the return of solar energy. No matter where you are based, honour Beltane as an opportunity to express joy. Light a candle or a bonfire, gather with your friends, dance and be merry!

GET TO KNOW YOURSELF

As with everything, you can't have what you don't know, so get to know what joy means to you. This month, spend some time unpacking whether any limitations you might be experiencing in cultivating joy are because of your limitations to feeling other emotions.

In order to truly connect with other people, places, life and joy, you must allow *all* your emotions to move through your experience. Acknowledging that *all* feelings are valid is essential when seeking to experience more joy.

Manifesting joy doesn't mean the absence of experiencing sadness. We all experience a range of emotions. When you deny your truth, suppress your emotions, or numb your essence, it creates disharmony within you and can block you from truly experiencing anything, including joy. Emotions are energy, and each can be seen as a signpost or indicator as to what is important to you. Acknowledging and healthily expressing all feelings is essential for your physical, mental and emotional health. You will only feel more joy if you allow yourself to feel.

Spend some time in quiet reflection this month,
journaling the following questions:

✧ What does joy mean to me?

✧ What 30 things do I find
delight in?

✧ Where do I feel joy in my body?

✧ What colour would I assign
to joy?

✧ What would greater joy look like
in my life?

✧ How could I cultivate more joy?

✧ What is blocking me from
experiencing joy? What thoughts
or beliefs do I have about joy?
What emotions do I struggle to
express or keep suppressed?

✧ What held my fascination as a
child? What sparks my curiosity
still?

✧ Is my self-talk, beliefs, thoughts
and words aligned with my
pursuit of joy or more?

A STORY OF A LONG AND JOYFUL LIFE

Gwen Culver, from Somerset, UK, celebrated her 100th birthday in 2022. Gwen lived through World War II as a land girl, before raising a family and working alongside her husband as a market gardener. She still lives independently, cooks her own meals and only very recently has given up responsibility for her garden. Gwen is undoubtedly young at heart and has a playful, joyful character with a wicked sense of humour, and her friends all agree that they never hear her complain. Gwen has manifested a long and joy-filled life, drawing strength and spiritual connection from nature. She has always prioritised finding gratitude in the simple things. In more recent years, talking to her grandchildren and great- grandchildren brings the biggest sense of joy in her life, alongside recalling joyful memories of the past, particularly the dances that took place in the village hall when she was a land girl. Gwen believes joy can be found in the simplest of things, especially in nature, watching birds and animals play or watching a garden grow.

Gwen attributes her long and happy life to her mindset, which has always been to work hard and to be kind to others, as well as to her connection to the earth through growing and eating vegetables. Her playful, young-at-heart mindset has helped her accept the inevitable changes in life with grace and to always look forward to the future. Gwen radiantly admits to having a great sense of gratitude for all that has been, what is right now, and all that is yet to come.

Change your mind

The link between joy, happiness and health (both mental and physical health) has been a keen area of interest for psychologists and neuroscientists for decades. A study titled 'Joy as a Virtue' carried out in 2020 concluded that joy is a dynamic process that perpetuates the ability to thrive. As with Gwen, you need to 'decide' to bring more joy into your life. This dynamic process requires self-growth and development. Manifesting joy is a dynamic process of play, curiosity and merriment. It requires honouring and savouring the simplest of things, finding awe and wonder in the magical, mystical journey of life and rejoicing in your blessings.

Manifesting joy also requires handing over the need for control and outcome, and instead enjoying the dynamic process of your life unfolding, with trust that you are always being supported.

AFFIRMATIONS FOR JOY

Repeat the following affirmations out loud to help reprogram your subconscious mind to notice and experience greater joy:

- ✧ I take time to delight in the simple things
- ✧ Joy is the essence of who I am
- ✧ I keep the experiences that bring me joy alive through my awareness and remember them in times of struggle
- ✧ I remember to see the world with childlike curiosity and awe
- ✧ I am worthy of experiencing joy
- ✧ It is safe to express joy
- ✧ It is safe to be myself completely

✧ A tea ritual to arouse ✧ joy from within

This month, practise this refreshing tea ritual, which uses natural herbs associated with helping you feel good. Tea rituals are found in most ancient cultures, usually using plants native to the area. Pagan tea rituals tend to suggest stirring clockwise when you wish to draw something in, and anti-clockwise when you wish to dispel something. Perform this ritual during daylight hours at the start of the month, then repeat again at the end of the month.

You will need

Yellow candle
1 tbsp dried lemon balm loose-leaf tea
1 tbsp dried St John's Wort loose-leaf tea (do not use this if you are pregnant, breastfeeding or on medication)
1 strip of lemon peel
1 strip of orange peel
1-2 tsp raw, local honey
Hot water
Your favourite cup
Paper
Coloured pens, pencils or paints
A short piece of yellow ribbon or string

1. Light your candle and set the intention to arouse joy from within.

2. Prepare the tea by stirring the tea, peels and honey in a bowl with boiling water, clockwise. Infuse it with feelings of gratitude and appreciation as you stir. You might like to whisper a prayer or simply the words 'thank you for my

blessings' before straining it into your favourite cup.

3. As you allow the tea to cool, gaze at your candle for 3-5 minutes. Allow your gaze to stay on the flame, the radiant dance of energy. Imagine it feeding the light and energy of joy and vibrancy within you.

4. When the tea is cool enough, sip it slowly, reflecting on all the things you are grateful for and find simple delight in. Receive the blessings you poured into the tea.

5. Now write out, draw, sketch or paint all the things you are grateful for (as many as you can find) on the piece of paper. Add a list of small delights.

6. When you are finished, roll the piece of paper up into a scroll and tie it with the yellow ribbon or string, then stub out the candle.

7. Place the scroll on a windowsill in direct sunlight for the remainder of the month.

8. At the end of the month, repeat the ritual, either adding to the existing piece of paper or with a fresh blank piece of paper.

9. Keep both rolled up somewhere safe, and if you ever need a boost of positivity, open them up to receive the blessings.

☾ ☾ ☾ ○

CHOOSE A SYMBOL FOR THIS MONTH

Joy and playfulness go hand in hand. Adopting a
childlike sense of curiosity might help
you slow down enough to notice the magic found
in the mundane or to delight
in the simple things.

Choose a symbol that evokes a feeling
of joy within you, and let that symbol act
as a reminder to play and delight in the
simple things this month.

You can sketch the symbol or find
an image and display it somewhere
you will see it often, to remind you of your
intention to experience joy.

HUMMINGBIRD

Perhaps due to the fact that hummingbirds are able to fly upside down and backwards, they are considered a symbol for playfulness and joy. Their ability to fly long distances and dart from flower to flower in search of nectar means they also symbolise resilience, freedom and the ability to take change in their stride in the pursuit of their desires. Rather charmingly, in ancient feng shui, a hummingbird picture hung in a baby's nursery was considered to bring the baby good luck. The hummingbird, and its appreciation of flowers and beauty, reminds us to pay attention to and appreciate the simple things.

THE COLOUR YELLOW

Thanks to its association with the sun, yellow is the colour most associated with joy, happiness, optimism and playfulness. The colour yellow represents the solar plexus chakra in the body, the space just above the belly button and below the ribs. This is the centre for self-esteem, joy, vibrancy and playfulness. If energy is blocked in this chakra, you might experience low self-esteem, victimhood mentality, repressed anger and poor digestion. In feng shui, yellow is a colour of luck and prosperity.

EUPHROSYNE

In Greek mythology, the goddess Euphrosyne represents joy, laughter and playfulness. Her role was to spread joy and good tidings. She is often depicted in paintings dancing and playing with nymphs, the personification of nature, usually in a beautiful female form.

Visualise this

Positive visualisation can be particularly helpful at times when you are feeling low and need a joy boost. Manifesting joy is about conjuring up the feeling of joy from within. Joy does not depend on external circumstance, although totems, events, and visualisations can help stir and evoke the feeling of joy residing within. Therefore, the act of visualising yourself joyful and thriving will help lift your mood, and will likely produce a better outcome.

In the liminal state, as you are drifting off to sleep this month, visualise yourself experiencing joy, delighting in the journey, and feeling a sense of awe at the natural world and the simple pleasures that life can bring.

Raise your vibration

Joy is a highly magic vibration. It not only feels good to you, but it also ripples and radiates out to others, helping them to feel good too. When you are living in a state of joy, you can enjoy a free, almost fearless state of being. It is easier to trust the unfolding, to playfully dance around the roadblocks or challenges, and to savour and delight in the view along the way.

To raise your vibration to joy this month – PLAY! Invite your inner child forward to play with and through you. Splash in puddles, search for shells or heart-shaped rocks on the beach, sing, watch the sunset, dance, watch comedy, laugh with your friends, make a mess or make a noise!

Joy is a high-vibrational state of living and being, and is actually the most natural vibration state for all of us. Vibing high when you have been used to embodying lower vibrational states such as confusion, sadness, grief or frustration (natural states we all experience and move through from time to time) can sometimes take a bit of practice and fine-tuning. Visualising the gradual dynamic process is crucial. You might like to imagine raising your vibration up to a frequency of joy, like turning up the volume on your speaker. Imagine gradually raising the volume so as to allow the body and mind to stay aligned, so you can enjoy, rather than feel overwhelmed, by this new vibrational experience.

A MEDITATION FOR JOY

Light a candle or some incense and set yourself up for an aligning, joy-inviting chakra meditation.

Sit upright, either on a chair or on the floor. Take a few deep breaths.

Become aware of the pillar of balance and energy of your spine, connected down into the earth and up into the cosmos. Take your awareness to the root chakra (the space at the base of your spine and pelvis) and imagine the colour red. Allow every easy breath in to connect you to this space in your body and to the colour red. Close your eyes as you do this.

Allow your awareness to move up slightly to the space below your belly button, your sacral chakra. Imagine the colour orange filling this space.

Next, bring your awareness up to the solar plexus, the space above your belly button and below your ribs. Imagine filling this space in the body with breath and the colour yellow.

Move your awareness up to the heart chakra, and fill the cavity of your chest with the colours green or pink.

Next, raise your awareness up to rest for a few moments on the throat chakra, imagining the colour blue.

Now draw your awareness to the space between your eyebrows (your third eye) and imagine the colour indigo filling this space.

Finally, allow your awareness to rest on the top of your head, the crown chakra, for a few breaths, visualising a pure white, beautiful light.

With all your chakras awakened and aligned, take your awareness back to the solar plexus, and the radiant yellow colour. Imagine every breath in is fed the joyful colour yellow. You might like to repeat the affirmations found on page 96 or simply affirm: 'I allow joy . . . I am joyful.'

When you are ready to close the meditation, connect back to the earth and the cosmos before bringing all your awareness back into the whole body and putting a smile on your face.

The joy of sunflowers

Beautiful, big, bright sunflower heads are the perfect attraction for busy bees. The sunflower characteristically turns its face towards the sun, reminding us to do the same. Joy seems to radiate from the sunflower, making it the perfect totem for joy. Sunflowers were traditionally used by Native American cultures for medicinal purposes, due to their antioxidant and anti-inflammatory compounds. The juice of their stem was often applied to heal wounds, and water infused by the flowers was used to treat kidney complaints.

This month, buy yourself some sunflowers or sow some sunflower seeds to grow at home. Display them somewhere prominent in your home and allow them to act as a reminder to turn your face towards the light and allow joy to radiate from you.

Understand the law of correspondence

The law of correspondence suggests the link between your inner and outer selves? alongside your relationship with the divine. Joy is an exact match to the higher spiritual energies, and is aligned with divine wisdom. The law of correspondence suggests that the outer world is merely a mirror image of the inner world – therefore, joy begins within.

May's practice

Keep a journal of delight. At the end of the day before you get into bed, jot down the simple things that brought you a sense of delight and joy this month.

Spend a few moments before your drift off to sleep visualising joyful experiences yet to come, as instructed on page 101.

06

MATERIAL DESIRES

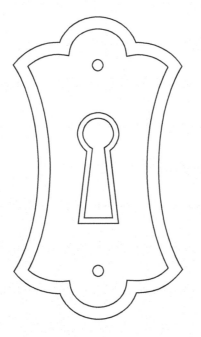

JUNE

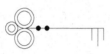

'IF IT MAKES YOU FEEL GOOD, IS
ALIGNED WITH YOUR GREATER
PURPOSE AND YOU ARE TAKING
PROACTIVE STEPS TOWARDS
ACHIEVING IT, YOUR WISH CAN
COME TRUE'

There is nothing wrong with manifesting material things if the item will truly enhance your life. If an object will bring you lasting or immeasurable joy, is in line with your purpose, or it will facilitate your manifestations in other areas of your life, then this is the chapter for you. For example, if you wish to write a book but don't own a decent laptop, manifesting one would make a lot of sense. If you have been driving an old, unreliable car and worry every time you turn the key that it won't start, manifesting a new, safe, reliable car would be an excellent use of your energy. Perhaps you need some good old-fashioned adventure – manifesting a train ticket to somewhere new sounds like a lot of fun.

However, this comes with a caveat. The constant manifestation of material things can lead to accumulation. With all the 'stuff' in the world, either you or landfill has to store it! If your focus is solely on the material, let's say money, you will never truly quench the thirst of satisfaction and experience the broader transformation that holistic manifestation enables. For a short while material items can make you feel good and in alignment, but then a few days/weeks/months later, the feeling wears off and your attention is onto the next shining thing you want to acquire to make you feel good.

Rhonda Byrne's iconic book, *The Secret* (2006), was groundbreaking at the time, as it propelled the concept of the law of attraction into the mainstream. It sold millions of copies worldwide, yet hasn't gone without criticism, mostly due to the focus being placed so heavily on manifesting materialism. Many have since tried to set the record straight about the deeper, more holistic view of manifesting. If you want to write a book, *you* still have to write it. Waiting for a shiny new laptop might be a block in disguise. Instead, you could use a library computer or even start with a pen and paper! Taking action demonstrates to the universe you mean business and will undoubtedly be rewarded.

June brings the longest day of the year in the northern hemisphere, which is marked by the summer solstice. It also brings the shortest day and the winter solstice in the southern hemisphere. Each celebration marks a pivotal time in the year when light gives way to the darkness, and darkness once again welcomes the light. Both teach us of the cyclical nature of all things and the unrelenting relationship between the seen and the unseen. In order for the new to be welcomed in, we must let go of the old to create space for it. Material manifestations exemplify this change, manifesting a new home, for example, and offer a poignant reminder to allow this to be a flow of transformation, and not accumulation.

GET TO KNOW YOURSELF

Understanding the deeper desires that drive your want for a material object can help you ascertain if it is really a feeling you are seeking, or the material item itself. For example, is it really designer clothes that you want to manifest, or a feeling of self-confidence? Exploring these desires also draws the object closer into your reality and unblocks any energetic resistance you might have preventing you from receiving it.

Journal the following prompts over the next month:

✧ List all of the material items you wish to manifest.

✧ What are your deeper beliefs about materialism?

✧ Do you feel worthy of receiving the items you desire?

✧ What are your beliefs about the possibility and chances of manifesting your material desires?

✧ How would the material items you wish to manifest benefit your life, the planet and others?

✧ Reflect on whether the material object you desire is actually a feeling you are seeking, or a true life improvement.

A STORY OF A PICTURE-PERFECT HOME

Anna Findlay had a dream of one day living by the sea in Penzance, Cornwall. She would visit as often as she could with her husband and family for holidays, driving the six hours it took from their home. On one visit, she purchased a big poster of a scene of Penzance, overlooking rooftops, out to the harbour and with St Michael's Mount in the distance. She placed the poster in a frame and hung it on her therapy room wall, in pride of place. Six years rolled by and it was time for her to turn her energy and attention to manifesting her perfect home. She visualised it, wrote out what she wanted and set the wheels in motion to make the move to Cornwall.

It wasn't until she moved into her beautiful home and hung her artwork on the walls that she realised the magic. She stood looking at the poster of Penzance she had bought years earlier, now hung on her new living room wall, and gasped! She took one step to the left and looked out at the view from her patio doors – the view identically matched that of the poster; overlooking rooftops, out to the harbour and with St Michael's Mount in the distance.

Change your mind

Have you ever had the experience where you recently bought something, or something new comes into your awareness, and all of a sudden you see that thing everywhere? I remember my mum saying she experienced this when she was pregnant – all of a sudden it seemed to her as if there were pregnant women everywhere. This can be explained scientifically as 'frequency illusion', which is a process that involves confirmation bias and selective attention, also known as the Baader-Meinhof effect. The experience helps us to understand that our physical reality reflects our thoughts, desires and biases. The subconscious mind is extremely good at noticing patterns. By imagining yourself with a material item you desire, it evokes a cognitive sense of physical ownership, assisting the subconscious mind to filter information aligned with your bias and desire – almost like clearing the path to your desire manifesting.

You can practise this with something trivial at first – cars are a common place to start. Imagine and visualise a specific colour or make of car to bring it into your conscious awareness, then go about your day. You might just be amazed at how many you see. The practices throughout this chapter will help you to utilise this cognitive fiction in order to manifest your material desires. You will need to be very clear on what material item you would like to manifest and let the Baader-Meinhof effect start to play out.

AFFIRMATIONS FOR MATERIAL DESIRES

Repeat the following affirmations out loud to help draw in what you want:
✧ I am worthy of my desires coming true

✧ I surround myself with things that bring me joy and aid my mission to feel good and do good

✧ I attract good things in my life

✧ I deserve . . . [an item or object you wish to manifest]

✧ I notice the beauty and the gifts that already surround me

✧ It is OK to ask for what I want

✧ I allow myself to be comfortable and happy

Call in specific items with this gratitude practice

Write a list of all the material things you would like to manifest as a gratitude list (you can use the list you created in the journaling section on page 109 if you like). They key is to write each out as if you already have them. Include how having that thing makes you feel, and what gift it is, and how it has enhanced your life. For example, if you would like to manifest a new car, write: 'Thank you for my new, reliable car. I love how safe I feel in it, it smells so good inside and I love how clean, fresh and new everything is. I love that it is better for the environment and that I can use renewable energy to fuel it. I feel so excited whenever I get to drive it, and the bright blue colour feels so me! Thank you, thank you, thank you for my car.'

Next, write a list of all the material items you already have. Write out, in a similar way, why you're grateful for them. For example, 'Thank you for my bed; it is so comfortable and feels so luxurious to get into each night' or 'Thank you for these boots – they are my absolute favourites. They are so comfortable, and look great too' or 'Thank you for my smartphone. It enables me to keep in touch with family overseas and I love that I can take high-quality pictures with it.'

CHOOSE A SYMBOL FOR THIS MONTH

Set the intention at the start of the month for the symbol, art or image that represents the object or item you'd like to manifest. Let it come to you as a sign. When you see it, you will know it is the right one! It might be a poster, a greetings card, a magazine cover . . . something that represents a physical manifestation of what you desire. When it finds you, purchase it if you are able or take a photo of it on your phone and print the picture. Frame it and hang it on your wall, just as Anna did, in your home or office. Let it be there, without obsessing over it or forcing the manifestation. Keep this as a symbol of your desire, alive and activated by it simply being displayed proudly and visibly for all to see.

MANIFESTING A PROJECT

Before my first book was published, I performed a ritual every time I went into Truro, the nearest town to where I live. No matter the reason for my visit (to meet a friend for coffee, to go to the post office or to work from a café for the afternoon), I would always go into the bookshop, make my way upstairs to the self-help section on the first floor, and I would visualise my 'one day' book on the shelves. I repeated this ritual every time I visited town, without fail, over the course of four years. I performed the ritual so many times it had become habitual.

One day, I entered the bookshop, as I always would, and made my way up to the first floor. My hand rose to my mouth and I gasped – there it was! Happily perched on the shelves of the self-help section was my first published book, just as I had imagined it.

Set yourself your own physical ritual, something you can perform like this, that will encapsulate your purpose manifested into a material item. Imagine your artwork hanging in your local gallery when you walk past or the jewellery you make being worn by your favourite pop star. Imagine seeing yourself on the billboard poster for a West End musical or seeing your book on the shelves of your local bookshop, just as I did. With time, patience, action, synchronicity and resilience, it will come true.

Raise your vibration

Manifesting your desires, including material items, doesn't happen overnight. But if it makes you feel good in the process, is aligned with your greater purpose and you are taking proactive steps towards achieving it, your wish can come true. The secret sauce that should be added to any manifesting practice is gratitude. Gratitude and appreciation facilitate fizzy feelings of positive expectation, optimism and passion. Have you ever been so grateful and excited about something that your eyes have welled up with joy and appreciation? It feels so good! When you are in a state of true gratitude, your vibration is magnetic.

Raise your vibration through gratitude this month by simply saying thank you for everything. Have a go! Say thank you to the bill that you paid, to the bike that you cycle, to the kindness you receive. If you come across something that truly does feel delicious, say thank you and then add 'more of this, please'. As podcast host Michael Sandler often says, add in: 'Something like this, or better'. The universe is listening.

I want to say a few things about 'feeling guilty' and toxic positivity. Do you ever think or say things like: 'I *should* be grateful for X, Y, Z' when comparing your life or circumstances to others? You might feel you *should* be grateful for your lot. Even though you might be trying to convince yourself and others that you are #grateful, you feel even worse about yourself and your situation for denying your true feelings. Esther Hicks puts it perfectly in her book *Ask and It Is Given* (2004), telling us that we can't just put a smile on our faces and cover up how we're really feeling. Hicks explains:

> If your fuel tank is low, you wouldn't simply cover it up with a happy face sticker because you didn't like seeing it. You would attend to it and take some action to remedy it. The same can be said for your emotions. Pretending you don't feel something doesn't change your vibration or make you feel any better, in fact, the disconnection can make you feel even worse.

Gratitude doesn't take the challenges or the pain away, but it can help bring about a greater sense of balance and optimism. There is always something to be grateful for, and remembering this can offer a sense of balance, hope and energy – there is so much good to come.

MEDITATION TO APPRECIATE
THE VALUE OF THINGS

As we have explored, manifesting material desires is not about accumulation, waste or mindless consumerism but about enhancing your life, assisting with your purpose, and celebrating joy. To appreciate the value of material objects and to remember the natural source of all things, practise this meditation with a piece of in-season fruit this month. Select a piece of fruit before you begin your meditation – perhaps an orange, apple or mango, depending on where you are.

Get into a comfortable seated position, close your eyes and take a few deep breaths. Take as long as you need to feel grounded and centred.

When you are ready, pick up the piece of fruit and take your gaze to it. Let it be a gaze of soft fascination; notice its colour, texture, shape and the intricate detail. Notice how it is perfectly imperfect. Notice the energy that it carries and the story that it tells. Reflect on the journey it has been on to be in your hands. Really take your time and let the simple piece of fruit be the object of your meditation.

When you are ready to finish your meditation, place the fruit down and close your eyes. Fill your body with breath, and smile.

How to anoint a talisman

A key has been an amulet of unlocking success, health, wealth, love and luck for centuries. When you're manifesting your physical desires, the key can symbolise the unlocking of the subconscious mind to access greater freedom, and it represents access to your new physical reality. If you want to manifest a new home or a new car, the key talisman is also an obvious choice to help you. Do this ritual on the new moon, at night-time.

You will need

Smudging stick
A key (old, new or ornamental – as long as
it isn't being used)
A green tea light
Clary sage essential oil
1 tsp dried or fresh rosemary

1. Smudge the space you are in, and also the key. Light the green tea light to signify the start of the ritual.

2. Hold the key in both hands and bring to mind a physical item you wish to manifest. Spend some time in meditation, feeling into the joy and appreciation having this item would bring you. Visualise yourself using it, wearing it or holding it.

3. Place the key down in front of you and sprinkle a few drops of the clary sage oil over the key and say out loud: 'I give permission for my subconscious mind and beliefs to align with my desire for [state the item you are manifesting].

4. Sprinkle the rosemary over the key and say: 'Let my desire to receive [the item] be loud and

clear as I co-create with the universe.'

5. Place the key and the tea light on a windowsill under the light of the full moon. Once the tea light has burned out by itself, the spell will be cast.

6. Keep the key in your wallet, bag, car, or on a windowsill, or hold as a talisman during your meditations this month.

Understand the law of expectation

The law of expectation is a self-fulling prophecy suggesting that what you expect, you receive. According to psychiatrist and hypnotherapist Dr Milon Erikson, 85 per cent of what you expect to happen does. Your expectations affect your behaviour, your decision-making, your energy and your vibration. However, the law states that you can't pretend to expect something in an attempt to convince or influence the law. It is your subconscious expectations – your deeper expectations – that influence the law and the outcome.

To become aware of your subconscious expectations and beliefs, take an inventory of them through quiet reflection this month. It could be something small, like your expectation for how the traffic will be on your bus journey, or something more significant, like how someone is going to treat you. Then take an inventory of what unconscious beliefs or expectations might be running the show. Once you have brought what is unconscious up into conscious awareness, you can then start to be healed, processed and changed.

June's practice

Whether you are basking in the summer sun in the northern hemisphere or cosying up with a hot tea in the south, spend five consecutive days this month practising this 55 x 5 manifestation ritual. This is an age-old manifesting practice to help reprogram your subconscious, filter information and attract what it is you desire.

Once a day, without fail, over the course of five days this month, write out your desires in a succinct, clear way and in present tense, 55 times. For example: 'I want a home of my own.'

Once you have completed the five days, surrender your desire to the universe and take action in other ways.

Pay particular attention if the number 555 shows up for you this month.

07

SUCCESS

JULY

'SUCCESS ISN'T ABOUT AN ARRIVAL OR ACCOLADE; INSTEAD, IT IS THE AMOUNT OF JOY AND FULFILMENT YOU FEEL ALONG THE WAY.'

The masculine definition of success we've been used to for centuries is about being the 'best' at something, recognition and domination. I believe the collective definition of success is shifting, as the divine feminine rises, seeking balance and harmony in the universe.

The universe is always expanding, and so are you and your desires! The process of manifestation doesn't have an end point. As one desire actualises, you will most likely find that it evolves, and a more expanded version emerges. This is not a bad thing; quite the opposite. It allows the universe to play and co-create with you throughout your journey of life, and it allows you to bloom to your full potential.

Success is living true to your purpose. Perhaps for you right now, manifesting success might look like raising a happy, healthy, secure child. Or maybe it's to turn your passion project into a business. Perhaps it's healing your inner child, or overcoming great adversity. Long-term success might look like making a film or becoming a headteacher. Short-term success might look like having made it through the day with your sense of humour intact! Whatever it might be, success is personal, it is achievable and it is ever-evolving.

Success isn't about an arrival or accolade; instead, it is the amount of joy and fulfilment you feel along the way. It is acknowledging magical moments of expansion – those full-body 'yes!' moments. It isn't about the number of awards on your wall, the followers you have, or the amount of adoration or validation you receive from others. It is about your authentic self and how much joy you feel doing something. It's your contribution to your family, community and to the planet.

So then, how do you manifest more success? You grow and expand as a human being. In order to grow, you have to set clear intentions and continually work on staying true to your heart.

No matter where you live on the planet, make a ritual of sun worship this month by consciously connecting with the energy of the sun at sunrise or sunset. The sun symbolically represents life, energy, generosity and positivity. In tarot and other divination practices, the sun symbolises success and radiance. Sun worship has been present in all cultures across the globe, with solar energy often associated with divine masculine. People born in July are ruled by the sun, and are associated with confidence, focus and hard work. Let the rising and setting of the sun be your meditation. Imagine it illuminating your desires and giving energy and life force to each of them.

WHAT DOES SUCCESS MEAN TO YOU?

In order for you to manifest success, you need to be clear on what success means to you. This will help you to get a very clear lead on the direction of travel you want your life to go in. For years I had a dream of being a writer, but I didn't dare share my work for fear of judgement. Slowly stepping out of my comfort zone, I submitted an article to a blog site with millions of subscribers. I was at a friend's house for dinner when the email came in saying it was going to be published. I let out a little squeal and jumped for joy! I told my friend what had happened and their immediate response was: 'Are you getting paid for it?' I replied no. The friend proceeded to tell me that, since there wasn't a financial reward, it was hardly a success worth celebrating. I remember thinking to myself that she had no idea of the inner work I had to do to pluck up the courage to even share it in the first place. To me, it was a milestone of success that lit up a path before me, one that felt so good. That, for me, was success.

Spend some time in quiet reflection, journaling
your response to the following questions:

✧ What do you want?

✧ What is your own personal
definition of success?

✧ What are your personal goals in
your life right now?

✧ What actions can you take today
to step closer to your dream, and
out of your current comfort zone?

✧ What can you surrender and let
go of in order to draw your
dream closer?

✧ Looking back over the last ten
years, what are you most proud
of? Where would you place a
milestone on the path?

✧ Looking forward, what are your
intended milestones on the future
path?

A STORY OF MANIFESTING SUCCESS

Success for Thom Hunt was building something and then sharing it with others. In 2011, Thom was diagnosed with bowel cancer, aged just 28. After a year of treatment, his whole outlook on life, and what was important to him, changed. Having grown up on his grandparents' farm as a child, he had a calling to reconnect to nature in the rawest sense, and to create a space that facilitated that connection for others too.

Synchronicity played its part, and in 2013, he was granted custodianship of a remote, abandoned woodsman's cottage on the banks of the River Fal in Cornwall. The cottage was only accessible by foot, and had been left to ruin many years before. For three years Thom lived in the cottage alone, painstakingly restoring it and building new rustic structures by hand. During that time he reconnected to the land and communing with the forest was very much part of his own healing. His hard work and passion manifested into a thriving outdoor adventure experience, 7th Rise, enjoyed by many today. It was, and still is, a success.

Over time, Thom's personal desires evolved and his focus turned to raising a family. In 2022, he made the decision to allow the 7th Rise team to step up into director roles, as he began to step away. Success can be found in bringing a project to life, and also in letting it go.

Change your mind

Having a 'growth mindset' is an essential component of any form of manifesting. The way you think about yourself and your circumstances, and the effort you put in, has a direct correlation with success. If you are experiencing hardship right now, it is understandably hard to believe that things will get better or that magical things are possible for you, but they are, and they will – I promise.

A growth mindset (the opposite of a fixed mindset) involves cultivating resilience while enjoying the process of growing and learning. It means knowing that change may take time but, with conscious enthusiasm and effort, it is possible. Success is about resilience, hard work, determination and the sheer amount of joy you feel while doing something. You might also have a positive impact on someone or something else.

The example of Eddie the Eagle

My favourite example of an amazing growth mindset is ski jumper Michael Edwards, otherwise known as 'Eddie the Eagle'. Eddie had a dream – he wanted to be a ski jumper and he wanted to compete in the Olympics, despite the UK not having a ski-jumping team. He had no financial backing, equipment or experience in the sport and was repeatedly told he couldn't do it. His defiant growth mindset led him to the Winter Olympics in 1988. He famously celebrated every run he completed with the same level of elation you might expect someone to display if they had come first – except he came last in every race. His love and passion for the process was infectious and he received media attention from around the world. His inspiring contribution to the 1988 games was signalled by the president of the Olympic committee mentioning Eddie in his closing ceremony speech (despite Eddie coming last).

AFFIRMATIONS FOR SUCCESS

Repeat the following affirmations out loud to yourself to help manifest success:

◇ Change is possible for me

◇ I am worthy of living a life I love

◇ Every day, I am learning something new

◇ I am always evolving, just as nature is around me

◇ I am worthy of success

◇ I am confident, strong and flexible and I can handle anything

Earth magic ritual

This ritual is about cultivating desires and success. Spend some time performing a planting ritual this month, connecting with Mother Earth. We bury and plant with the same hands, into the same earth. The old becomes fertiliser for the new. As you let go of old thought patterns, a fixed mindset, or old ways of being, you create space to move forward on your journey closer towards the next milestone. Just as the sun helps plants to grow, shining the light of awareness onto your dreams helps your experience of success to grow too. This ritual takes about an hour. You will need to find a quiet space outdoors, such as a forest, wood or your own garden.

You will need

2 pieces of plain, untreated, recycled paper, and pen
A spoon

---

1. If possible, mindfully walk barefoot to your outdoor destination.

2. Sit comfortably, and practise a short meditation to ground and centre yourself.

3. Consciously connect with the natural elements around you. Notice water, birds and trees, and let the sounds or sights be your meditation. Reflect on the perfection of each individual bird, the effortless flow of the river, or the strength and wisdom of the trees.

4. Reflect on your personal journey in life and consider what it is you are ready to bury. Write it on one of the pieces of paper. Reflect on the goals and aspirations you would like to manifest, and write them on the other piece of paper.

130

5. Fold each piece of paper up and dig a small hole in the ground with the spoon. Place both pieces of paper in the hole and cover it with soil, as you offer a sense of gratitude for what you are burying and planting, and to the earth for holding and alchemising them both.

6. Close your ritual by standing tall like a tree. Visualise roots connecting you to the earth. Raise your arms up over your head, like the branches of the tree, and feel your connection to the sky and the cosmos. Draw your hands down to place both palms over your heart and whisper: 'Thank you (to the past), thank you (to the future) and thank you (to the present moment).'

☾ ☾ ☾ ○

CHOOSE A SYMBOL
FOR THIS MONTH

This month you will be choosing your personal symbol, something that is relevant specifically to your own goals and aspirations, and is meaningful to you. Eddie the Eagle might have chosen the five interlocking Olympic rings, for example. Spend some time reflecting on what symbol would represent success to you, or invite the universe to give you a sign and bring a symbol into your awareness.

Find a picture of your symbol, or sketch it, or find a physical representation and display it somewhere you can see it this month, to remind you of your intention for personal success, to embody success and to draw the energy of success into your reality.

CREATE A FUTURE MEMORY SCRAPBOOK

Creating a scrapbook is a way of visualising your future success. Buy yourself a notebook that you really enjoy holding and looking at. Gather together images of all that you are calling in: the future milestones of your success, perhaps from magazines or clippings. Stick them down in your 'future memory' scrapbook. Make it pop with positivity! You might like to include images of the sun, bright yellow, etc. It should look and feel enticing, exciting and motivating when you peruse it.

Add to your scrapbook this month as and when you see an image of something that you want to add. You can add annotations, sketches and words that all represent your future memories – the desire you are calling in.

Raise your vibration

Your ability to thrive and vibe high also depends on what you are feeding your mind, body and soul. This month, be really conscious of what you are listening to, watching and consuming. Fear-based media and news is captivating and has the intention to keep you hooked in and watching. Unfortunately, it preys on societal anxieties and evokes a greater sense of stress, reporting only on the most extreme, catastrophic or tragic news. Even the films and television programmes you watch will have an effect on your nervous system and your subconscious biases. Make a conscious effort to consume content that is aligned with your goals and desires, and that supports your mental health.

Friends who uplift and inspire

Author Jim Rohn claims that you are the average of the five people you spend most of your time with. Your environment, and the company you keep, has a big impact on your success. So let's reflect on your top five people. List the five people you spend the most time with.

✧   What qualities and traits do they possess?

✧   How do you feel when you hang out with them? Do you feel energised or drained after spending time with them?

This exercise doesn't intend to suggest you turn your back on friends who are having a hard time or in need, but just to consciously become aware of how you spend your energy, and what affect others have on you. Some people champion your growth and expansion, while others tend to drain you of energy and enthusiasm. Growth, expansion, energy and enthusiasm are all essential ingredients for success. Perhaps you might need to set some healthier boundaries with those who take more than they give, or manifest an inspiring, more supportive group of friends (see April's chapter, on community).

CLEANSE YOUR SPACE FOR SUCCESS

Is the space you work or spend most of your time in inspiring and clean? Can you set up a sacred space in your home to work on your passion project? Perhaps you could include a plant or display your chosen symbol for July on your desk in the office.

I remember getting into a friend's car once, and it was immaculate. She had a small bunch of fresh flowers hanging on the rear-view mirror, and gorgeous throws on each seat. I commented on how remarkable it was, and she replied: 'I drive so much for work, this is my office! I want to make it as comfortable and inspiring as possible so I'm in the best headspace each day.'

Love your body

The food you eat has its own vibration. Living foods, such as fresh fruit and vegetables, are considered high-vibration foods. Processed food is considered low vibration. In addition to eating well, you need to keep yourself hydrated. Also, regularly moving your body, getting adequate rest and good-quality sleep will all affect your vibration. This month, aim to get outside more, be active and eat delicious salads and vegetables. Every change you make today, in alignment with your desires and towards your goals, will help move you nearer to them, and it will feel good in the moment too. Win-win.

A MEDITATION FOR SUCCESS

Meditation has been proven to increase focus, attention, confidence, energy and clarity – all very important aspects in achieving success in any area of your life. Meditating for success doesn't require any striving or straining. In fact, it requires the opposite – complete surrender. All the magic takes place in letting go, relaxing the mind and body and attuning to deeper levels of consciousness.

This Box Breathing practice will help you to regulate your mind, body and soul. You can also do this when you need to feel calm, perhaps before an interview, a presentation, or when about to perform.

Set a timer for 5 to 10 minutes. Sit comfortably, and when ready, close your eyes. Slowly inhale to the count of four. Hold your breath for the count of four. Slowly exhale to the count of five. Repeat for 5 to 10 minutes.

A talisman for success

Your talisman for this month is simple yet powerful: a moonstone crystal. Let it be a reminder of your growth mindset, of your intention for joy and to serve others. Let
it be a reminder that you are on a journey and you are doing great exactly as and where you are. You can simply hold a moonstone during meditation, or you can wear it in a necklace cage or macrame holder. Alternatively, you could find a piece of jewellery – a broach or accessory – that houses a moonstone crystal.

You will need

A moonstone crystal

1. Wear or hold a moonstone crystal as a talisman for personal success this month.

Real success

In his book, *Ecological Literacy* (1992), environmental scientist David Orr said: 'The planet does not need more successful people. But it does desperately needs more peacemakers, healers, restorers, storytellers and lovers of every kind.' Reading this, I believe he could be referring to success in the old patriarchal sense and, if so, I agree.

If you are in a personal tower of success, but the village and earth beneath you are burning, is that really success? You are a reflection of the natural world, and are as successful as the community and environment that surrounds you. Personal success is only meaningful if it has a positive impact on the natural world, on those we love, or on humanity. Living in harmony with the earth and being of service to the planet is the essence of earth magic and successful evolution.

As nature evolves and the universe expands, we must consider our own expansion working in harmony with it. Sometimes miraculous leaps of progression happen, in nature and in our own lives, in an unimaginably short space of time. We call these occurrences miracles or quantum leaps. But often, things take time to evolve – some things longer than others. If you focus on finding the joy in the process and you're enthusiastic about learning and growing for the sake of it, not for an outcome, the length of time won't matter because you're doing good and having fun.

If you feel that progress is slow, imagine 'zooming out' so you are able to observe from a distance the whole journey of your life. Look at the hardships and challenges you have already overcome, and the milestones of success you have staked in the ground along the way. There are many more experiences you are yet to have, people you are yet to meet and future milestones you have yet to proudly mark along your path.

July's practice

A morning ritual is essential for setting your day up for manifesting success. Morning routines are encouraged by the ancient sages of Vedic practices and modern-day billionaire tycoons alike! How you set your day up will have a huge impact on your state of mind, your energy and your focus. It is the difference between starting your day in a whirlwind of scattered thoughts and energy and starting your day focused. Try this as early in the day as you can. Robin Sharma, author of *The 5am Club* (2018), suggests 5am, but work with what would truly be sustainable for you. You will need about half an hour.

Morning

Wake up early. Move for about 3 minutes – shake your body, stretch, jump up and down, all to get your circulation and serotonin flowing.

Now light a candle and get your journal out. Julia Cameron, author of *The Artist's Way* (1992), calls early morning journaling 'morning pages'. Write anything that comes to your mind, a brain dump of thoughts, whatever you need to write, for up to 10 minutes.

Now set a timer for 5–10 minutes, and simply sit quietly, focusing on your breath as explained on page 135.

08

ABUNDANCE

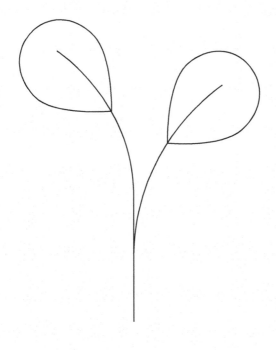

AUGUST

'NATURE IS THE GREATEST EXAMPLE
OF EMBODIED ABUNDANCE'

Manifesting abundance could be applied to almost every chapter in this book – luck, opportunities, love, self-love . . . In this chapter we are going to focus on bringing more magic, energy and attraction into our relationship with money.

Money is energy, and energy is the currency of the universe. It is a symbol of exchange and appreciation and should be celebrated and respected as such. Money, because it is energy, has to keep moving and changing form, and it is an instrument to help you experience your deeper desires. However, abundance is not really about how much money you have or don't have; it is about how abundant you feel within yourself. Those with very little financial wealth might live with a greater sense of well-being and gratitude than an extremely wealthy person with all the money in the world.

There is a difference between abundance and accumulation. Accumulation is destructive for the planet but also for the human spirit – it is the result of fear, that you might lose what you have, so you have to keep taking. We only need to look to Ebenezer Scrooge in the famous Dickens story *A Christmas Carol* to find an example of that embodied!

True abundance is bountiful, beautiful and generous. Nature, as always, is the greatest example of embodied abundance. The apple trees don't fill their branches with juicy ripe fruit only to keep the harvest for themselves. Manifesting money is much the same; it helps us experience our desire but it can also help us facilitate positive change for others and the planet. Abundance is generosity in disguise!

On 8 August (8/8) every year, the Lion's Gate Portal opens, offering a potent time to give thanks for your blessings and to manifest more abundance. This annual celestial event honours when the sun; Sirius (the brightest star in the sky); Orion's belt and the Earth come into alignment. It can be known as the Galactic New Year. For many, 8 August is the key day for manifestation, so mark it in your diary!

Take some time on the day to get super clear on what abundance you want – in any aspect of your life. Write it all down, speak it out loud and visualise your future, then hand it all over to the universe.

An abundant mindset

To embody abundance, you must believe there is more than enough of something to go around. A study carried out by the University of Pittsburgh in 2020 identified eight behaviours that impacted an abundance mindset: generosity, self-development, resilience, believing you deserve it, inclusion, risk-taking, thinking big and investing in yourself or others. So, this month, we will look at how you can do more of these! When you feel abundant, you might also feel a sense of personal safety and freedom, and then are more able to express greater generosity to others.

A lot of people are more practised in a scarcity mindset: a deep-seated, somewhat unconscious fear-based belief that there isn't enough to go around. It could be money, love, happiness or kindness, and so they make those things conditional and keep a tight grip on them in case they lose them. When you are in a scarcity mindset, you block the flow, and this will stop you manifesting what you desire.

GET TO KNOW YOURSELF

Our beliefs about money usually start in childhood. Was there a culture of belief in your childhood home that money was good, easy to come by and there is more than enough to go around? Was money considered useful, positive and a tool for generosity? Or did you grow up around the belief that money is the root of evil, that it was scarce and unobtainable, that people with money were somehow bad, and that it must be kept hold of for fear of it running out?

It is important to remember that this journaling practice is not about blame or guilt. When you have tasted real hardship, it is very understandable that you might fear being in the same situation again. A scarcity mindset doesn't make a person wrong, because poverty is unimaginably hard – I know, I have been there. In order to improve your relationship with money, and manifest more of it, you have to believe that your desire is possible and that you deserve it. You don't need to know exactly how it will show up, just that it unequivocally will.

Spend some time understanding your own beliefs – and blocks – by journaling the following reflection points throughout this month:

✧ What are your deeper beliefs about money? Where did those beliefs come from – parents, a past experience, your current situation?

✧ Why do you want to manifest more money into your life?

✧ How would having more money affect those around you?

✧ How does generosity feel, if you were to start today?

✧ What patterns are surfacing in your life about money?

✧ What comes up for you when you think about money? What is the predominant feeling – excited, calm, fearful or neutral?

A STORY OF
MANIFESTING WEALTH

Actor, Jim Carrey has frequently shared his own powerful manifestation story involving money. In the 1990s, before his career took off and he was completely broke, he would drive to the same spot every evening and visualise movie opportunities, offers and compliments about his work coming to him. To add to his visualisation, he wrote himself a cheque for ten million dollars, and dated it five years ahead for Thanksgiving in 1995, before stowing it away in his wallet. Just before that date, Jim Carrey made ten million dollars from *Dumb and Dumber* (a childhood favourite of mine!). He has since attributed his ability to manifest to not only believing that it was possible, but also putting dedicated hard work in to bring his visions to life. In 2005, 10 years later, Carrey set up the Better U Foundation with the mission to provide global food security. In 2009, he co-founded the Global Alliance for Transformational Entertainment, seeking to elevate loving and peaceful media content. He regularly gives to charity.

Change your mind

The words you speak, and think, are powerful. Words have vibrational power that is in constant communication with the universe, and they are also a clear indicator of your deeper inner beliefs about money. You are already practising and repeating affirmations all day long, whether consciously or unconsciously. Perhaps, for some, those affirmations might sound like 'I'm not good with money', 'I don't have enough money', 'money turns people bad', 'I can't afford it' or 'I don't deserve wealth'. When we tell ourselves or others something about ourselves, we are also telling the universe too.

When doing this work, I uncovered that I held a deep-rooted feeling of shame about money, and was somewhat proud of and attached to the identity I was embodying of a broke yet hard-working person. I started to notice that if someone gave me a compliment, such as 'I like your dress,' I would immediately deflect it by replying, 'Oh, this was only £10 from Asda.' Somewhere, deep down, I didn't believe I was worthy of abundance.

The stories we tell about money and our relationship to it shape our behaviour and how we feel when we have to spend money. It is only too common to feel resistant to paying for the boring stuff like bills or taxes, and worse still when you bury your head in the sand and try to ignore finances all together. In order to manifest more money, your relationship with it has to shift from fear to love. You can do this with simple mindset shifts and affirmations.

To manifest more money, you have to do something differently than you have done before:

✧   Start telling the story of your future, not your past.

✧   Make yourself a financial plan and seek help if you need to.

✧   Have a clear vision or goal and take conscious steps to get there.

✧ Pay attention to the words and stories you tell yourself and others about money. If you are complaining about money and telling yourself and your friends you can't afford something, you are telling the universe too.

AFFIRMATIONS FOR ABUNDANCE

Make a commitment this month (and beyond) to not speak negatively about money and to replace any negative thoughts and beliefs with these positive affirmations:

✧ Abundance flows easily to me

✧ I allow money to circulate and flow

✧ There is more than enough to go around

✧ I am abundant and grateful for the money I have

✧ Thank you for all the abundance I am about to receive

✧ I am good with money

A letter to the universe

You are going to write a letter to the universe, to call in abundance. Ideally, do this on this month's new moon, at night-time.

You will need

Smudging stick
A small green taper candle
Matches
Paper, envelope and a pen

1. Smudge your space and yourself. Close your eyes and take a few deep breaths. Set the intention to be focused for the next 10-15 minutes.

2. Imagine for a moment how it would feel to have your wish for abundance fulfilled. Feel the gratitude, appreciation, anticipation and freedom this might enable.

3. When you're ready, keeping that yummy feeling of appreciation in your heart, light the candle and pick up the paper and pen. Write the universe a letter; start by stating how much you would like to receive and by when. Continue by writing out all the things you will do with the money, the positive impact it would have on the lives of others, along with the practical steps you are going to take to assist in the co-creation of this manifestation. That might be networking, doing some work for free to gain experience or changing your inner beliefs about money and the way you speak and feel about it.

4. Close the letter by writing out one or more of the affirmations on page 147, three times. Write a future date on the envelope and place the letter in the envelope.

☽ ☽ ☽ ○

CHOOSE A SYMBOL
FOR THIS MONTH

For some, money itself is a symbol of abundance, but perhaps a symbol from the natural or metaphysical world that represents abundance more broadly might also resonate with you.

Choose an image of – or sketch – a symbol that represents abundance for you. You might like to find your own or choose one listed below. Display this symbol somewhere visual, so you will see it often, reminding you of your intention to feel abundant and to experience more synchronicities.

THE COLOUR GREEN

Green is the colour of nature's abundance, growth and fertility, and it is also a symbol of wealth and plenty. It is the colour associated with the heart chakra and is the colour of an American dollar bill. Wear green, paint your nails green and choose green this month to act as a symbol for your manifestations.

888

Angel numbers are a repeated set of numbers that are considered to be signs from the universe. Seeing the number 888 is a sign of wealth and good fortune, and it is an indication you are on the right track. According to numerology, numbers carry their own vibration. Keep your eyes peeled for spotting 888 this month, as confirmation that your desire to manifest money is being heard.

PIG

Have you ever wondered why you had a piggy bank when you were a child? Pigs are a symbol of good luck around the world. In Chinese culture, pigs are considered to be a symbol of wealth and good luck, while in Germany, you'll hear them say 'Glücksschwein', which translates to 'lucky pig!'

LAUGHING BUDDHA

A laughing Buddha is a small statue or talisman of a Chinese monk, wearing a robe and a huge smile on his face. Placing a laughing Buddha in your home is said to attract wealth and good fortune, especially depictions of him in which he is holding a ball.

Visualise this

It is a common phenomenon for big lottery winners to lose their fortune within a matter of years, simply because they were not prepared to manage or embody the wealth they inherited. Visualising your wealth before you receive it will help you resonate with wealth and attract it in, and also help you respect and energetically prepare space for the money that is coming to you.

Once a week this month, practise how it would feel to be wealthy through a deliberate visualisation practice. Spend some time in conscious daydreaming, visualising yourself as wealthy and generous. Notice how you might feel in your body and how you interact with others, as if it's happening in the here and now.

Imagine yourself setting up a trust, donating to charity or buying a loved one or other deserving person something they have longed for. Start to educate your nervous system, your thoughts and your inner beliefs, about how comfortable and expansive having the wealth you desire will be. Then let go and surrender your dream to the universe. Anchor yourself fully back into the present moment, but keep the feelings of generosity and contentment with you.

Raise your vibration

How do you feel when you pay for something? Do you have a prominent feeling of appreciation and gratitude as you transfer or hand over the money, or do you do so begrudgingly, with a feeling of dread? The thoughts you think and the beliefs you hold about money (as explored on page 143) affect your vibration, but the state in which you interact with money also plays a role. Here are some simple gratitude and mindfulness practices to shift your vibration for abundance:

✧ Every single time you pay for something, feel gratitude that you are able to. When you pay a bill, do so with gratitude, consciously taking note of the gift that bill brought about – keeping you warm or healthy, for example. If you're paying off debt or a credit card, make a list of all the things that money enabled you to do – perhaps to go on an adventure or even just to get by – and feel genuine gratitude for it.

✧ Be conscious of what you are spending your money on. Since money is energy, check in to make sure there is resonance between your inner values and beliefs and what you are purchasing. Feel good about spending money and when you are choosing to buy something. Make it a conscious choice and a moment of appreciation for you to enjoy and circulate good energy.

✧ Feel as if you already have abundance. How would abundance feel in this moment? What would you do if you had an abundance of money right now? How would it feel? How different would your day look? What would you do differently? Consciously feel into a state of abundance and embody it throughout your day. Step into the future as the future, rather than embodying the stories of the past.

✧ Practise generosity. Give without condition, or the expectation of recognition or reward. Cook something for someone struggling, pick flowers, donate to a cause that matters to you, pay for coffee when you meet up with a dear friend. Practise generosity within your means.

MEDITATION FOR ABUNDANCE

Set a timer for 10 minutes before getting into a comfortable position, preferably lying down. Close your eyes, and take a few calming deep breaths.

Take your awareness up to your third eye (the space between your eyebrows), and spend a few moments simply breathing, with your awareness on your third eye.

Start to imagine looking at your bank account, seeing it abundant with money. Imagine money as energy flowing to you and through you. Imagine the faces of those you would bless with your generosity.

Repeat the following affirmation quietly to yourself: 'I allow money to flow to me,' 'I enjoy being generous,' 'I am abundant and I am grateful.'

Take a big inhale, with a big smile on your face, and go about your day.

Find a talisman

Spend some time in nature this month, and collect an item that signifies abundance to you. Find your own symbol of abundance: perhaps a shell, fresh flowers or a leaf from an evergreen tree. Carry your talisman home in your hand and feel the vibration of abundance as you walk. Imagine the energy of gratitude, positive expectation and abundance transferring into your talisman.

Place your talisman somewhere prominent at home and let it act as a reminder to you to feel abundance, and a good luck charm to attract more abundance into your life.

Understand the law of attraction

The law of attraction suggests that like attracts like. What you put out into the universe, you get back. If you think positive thoughts, you attract good things. Much of what we have explored this month is based on this principle set out by the law of attraction – your thoughts, your words and your subconscious beliefs shape your reality.

However, to focus solely on thoughts, as it is popular to do in the field of manifesting, is an oversimplification, as it suggests that only our thoughts are responsible for manifesting our desires. This isn't quite the full picture and it is missing the magic! Manifesting is multidimensional. To manifest what you want in your life, you must be clear on what you want and believe it is possible. Focus on feeling good in the present and surrender the how and when to the universe. You cannot force or over-think them into being. The vibration of embodiment, trust, openness and receptivity that comes when you have clear intentions – that is law of attraction. Therefore, manifesting abundance certainly involves your thoughts, because repeated thoughts become beliefs. And when your beliefs about abundance change, that's when the magic really starts happening.

August's practice

This month we are focusing on the '3-6-9' manifesting method. The number three in numerology represents nobility and manifestation. Repeat these manifestations every day throughout this month. For added zest and magic, include something you are grateful for each day.

First, decide on a positive affirmation statement starting with 'I am.' For example, 'I am wealthy,' 'I am financially abundant' or 'I am good with money.'

Morning	Every morning before you get out of bed, write that positive affirmation out three times.
During the day	During the day, make time to write the same affirmation six times (six represents togetherness).
Evening	Just before bed, write your affirmation a further nine times (nine represents the cyclical nature of all things).

09

HARMONIOUS
RELATIONSHIPS

SEPTEMBER

'WHAT IF YOU LOVED ANYWAY?'

One thing is for certain - we cannot change other people, no matter how hard we try. The only thing we do have control over, or have the power to change, is ourselves. You might consider casting a spell to change someone else to meet your own preferences, but in doing so, you are wasting precious energy that you could be directing towards your own healing and transformation. Patterns will keep repeating in our lives until we have healed, changed or transformed wounded or hidden parts within ourselves. As you change, the relationships around you will change.

So, manifesting harmonious relationships is about changing your own mindset and tending to your own inner healing. Through the self-empowerment and awareness that comes from doing this work, you might find that you are more easily able to:

✧ set healthy boundaries

✧ communicate your needs, thoughts, feelings and fears more clearly

✧ stand up for yourself when needed

✧ be open to receive or to walk away from a relationship that is no longer serving you

✧ call in relationships that are more aligned (see page 71 on manifesting community).

Manifesting harmonious relationships requires you to consider the quality of your own interactions with people. Key to this is knowing that other people's behaviour, words or actions are never personal, no matter how personal it feels at the time. Whether there is disharmony or conflict at work, in your social circle or home life, other people's behaviour is a reflection of *their* own inner world, even if it feels like you are getting the brunt of it.

There is a famous Marianne Williamson quote from her beautiful book *A Return to Love* (1992) that explains: 'As we let our own light shine, we unconsciously give other people permission to do the same'. In order to manifest a change in relationship dynamics, you must embody the qualities and energy you wish to receive. In doing so, change will naturally occur around you, or you will feel more empowered to let a relationship go.

The autumn equinox, Mabon, is celebrated between 21 and 29 September each year in the northern hemisphere, celebrating the Green Man and the Goddess. Spring equinox celebrations take place in the southern hemisphere, celebrating Ostara, the goddess of spring and new beginnings. Both celebrations are centred about giving thanks for what has been and welcoming the new. As you set the intention to manifest more harmonious relationships this month, is it possible to give thanks for what has been and wipe the slate clean to welcome in the new?

GET TO KNOW YOURSELF

I remember taking a course a few years back and I was convinced that the course leader, whom I really respected, didn't like me. I interpreted everything that was said or done as if I was being singled out or that others were clearly being favoured over me. In a moment of awareness, I caught myself rehearsing these stories of victimhood and wrongdoing in my mind, and I decided to flip the story. I decided to believe that they did like me and that I was worthy and welcome on the course. I was able to identify that my deeply buried beliefs that I wasn't worthy or welcome had influenced my perspective.

When I switched my mindset, I experienced an instant shift in the way I felt, in our communication and my whole experience of being on the course. So much so that we went on to become great friends. The change in mindset gave me a greater sense of freedom and flow within me at the time, and I am sure altered the tone and quality of my communication to be more open and friendly, my energy to be more attractive, and I manifested a wonderful new friendship. If we genuinely wish to manifest a stronger relationship with someone, we must embody the energy we want to attract. Take out your journal and reflect on the following:

✧ Is your interpretation of a relationship based on perception or fact?

✧ What limiting beliefs might be contributing to the disharmony?

✧ How would it feel to give what you want to receive?

✧ Are you masking your true feelings in relationships?

✧ If you are dealing with a challenging relationship of any kind – at work, in your family, etc., what would you hope to receive from the other person?

✧ Are you giving out what you want to receive?

✧ What do you want?

A STORY OF CHANGING RELATIONSHIPS

Hardworking, fun-loving mum of two Becky recognised that she had a habit of overthinking in her life that wasn't supporting her sense of well-being. So she made a very conscious decision to try and turn negative thoughts into positive ones. With practice and dedication, she started to notice that life seemed to get a lot easier. She noticed positive changes started happening in her life; nuisance neighbours moved on, relationships improved and she was given a promotion at work.

To help process and manage a challenging relationship situation in her life, she joined a fellowship called Al-Anon, which supports family and friends of those affected by alcoholism. The key lesson she took away from the group was the life-changing ability to hand over challenges and problems to a higher power. The more she was able to do this, and detach from the things that caused her hurt and pain, the more she was able to manifest a sense of peace and harmony in her life and her relationships.

Change your mind

To manifest a positive change in your relationships, start by looking for things you appreciate in them, instead of all the things that are wrong. Give what you want to receive, ask for what you need and ask what they need in return.

AFFIRMATIONS FOR HARMONY

Repeat the following affirmations this month to help you along the way:

- ✧ It is OK to ask for what I need
- ✧ I am worthy of harmonious relationships
- ✧ I choose to be the love I seek
- ✧ Harmonious relationships are possible for me
- ✧ Boundaries show people how to love me
- ✧ It is safe for me to be myself
- ✧ I don't take other people's behaviour personally
- ✧ I set clear, loving and flexible boundaries

Challenging relationships

Being the change you wish to see in the world is unbelievably challenging when it comes to relationships, especially tricky ones. When we feel we are being wronged or not being treated to our liking, it is harder for us to remain open and loving. Hostility makes most people recoil or fight back; it is the activation of the innate fight or flight response, a survival mechanism that keeps us alert to, and safe from, danger. These days, it is often our ego's sense of identity that is being challenged, not our physical safety (if your physical safety is being threatened, seek support immediately).

If it is your sense of self that is being threatened, you have the power to alchemise it into healing. Manifesting harmonious relationships does not require you to become passive and allow mistreatment – quite the opposite. When you do the inner work to understand your limiting beliefs and expectations, and heal your inner wounds, you are more likely to get what you want because you're able to ask for it. You are more able to set healthy boundaries to receive what you desire. You might also grant yourself the permission to let toxic relationships go because you know your worth.

HONEY JAR SPELL

Use this spell to help 'sweeten' and to bring
freshness to any relationship in your life you wish
to enhance. Start this spell at the beginning
of the month.

You will need

Smudging stick
Pen and small piece of paper
A clear, clean jar with a lid
1 tbsp raw honey
1 tbsp lavender
3 fresh mint leaves
2 small cinnamon sticks (which will fit in the jar)
A pinch of chilli flakes
A small white candle

1. Smudge yourself and the jar before starting. Take a few long, slow, deep breaths and close your eyes.

2. Bring to mind the person you wish to sweeten your relationship with. Imagine them as their inner child if it helps build compassion. Start to imagine how it would feel to have an improved relationship with them. Use your imagination and intention to conjure up the feeling of harmony and peace you wish to feel.

3. When you are ready, write their name on the piece of paper and fold it up. Smudge the piece of paper before placing it into the jar.

4. Hold the feeling you are wanting to manifest as you add the honey to the jar, covering the paper. Add the lavender and mint, to add freshness to the relationship; the cinnamon sticks to represent the two of you; and the pinch of chilli to speed up the process. Holding the feeling you wish to manifest, seal the jar.

5. Next, take the candle and melt a little bit of wax from the bottom of the candle so you can stick it to the top of the jar lid. Once the candle is secure, take a moment to conjure up the feeling of harmony you are manifesting and light the candle.

6. Allow the candle to burn down. You may need to do multiple sittings over the course of the month to allow the candle to burn out on its own. Once it has, the spell will be cast. Remember, don't blow the candle out – otherwise, the spell will be cancelled. Instead, safely stub it out.

CHOOSE A SYMBOL
FOR THIS MONTH

Working with symbols works two ways: they can
remind you of your intention, and they can also
act as a means of communication between the
you and the universe, or your subconscious mind.
Setting an intention is often the easy bit.
Remembering our intentions when we are faced
with challenges, especially when it comes to
challenging relationships, is often the work.

By working with a symbol, and displaying it
somewhere you will see it often, it will help remind
you of your intention, keeping it in your conscious
awareness. And you never know, it might just pop
up when you most need the reminder!

YIN AND YANG

The popular yin and yang symbol represents balance and harmony between dark and light; night and day; negative and positive; and masculine and feminine. It shows the light embracing the dark and the dark embracing the light. This symbol represents the beauty and harmony that can be created when differences are welcomed.

WUNJO RUNE

A 'P'-shaped symbol, the rune Wunjo represents companionship and togetherness. It can also represent a need to change your perspective so that you see a situation with more clarity. It reminds us that if we want to experience joy, love and connection, we must be the energy of joy, love and connection and shift our mindset accordingly.

HARMONIA

Harmonia is the Greek goddess of harmony and unanimity. She had the power to soothe conflict and disharmony among people and in relationships.

DOLPHIN

Many legends and myths surround dolphins, particularly those of dolphins saving sailors out at sea. Dolphins are highly intelligent and social creatures. For these reasons, dolphins have become a symbol of harmony, protection, cooperation and playfulness.

THE NUMBER 2

The number 2 represents harmony, teamwork, balance and cooperation, so look out for it this month. Seeing 222 are these elements amplified. You might see this number when you are at a stage in your life where you need to make an important decision or change. It can also indicate a resolution of conflict. You can see the numbers 2, 22 or 222 as a symbol of teamwork and cooperation with the universe or with your personal relationships.

Visualise this

Practise this visualisation to rise above your current circumstances and release your emotions to the universe.

Take some time to prepare a comfortable space to perform this visualisation. Set up some cushions on the floor, play some soothing music and light some incense. When you are ready to begin, lie down comfortably on the floor.

Take a few rounds of deep belly breaths, breathing right down to your belly and sighing the breath out. Allow all the muscles of your body to relax. Place one hand over your heart and one hand over your belly. When you are relaxed and comfortable, start to visualise a safe, peaceful scene that looks out onto a horizon. This can be anything that works for you – a forest, a beach or a mountain view. Imagine standing in a safe and comfortable space with a view of the vast horizon.

Now imagine looking down into the palms of your hands and seeing an emotion as a ball of energy. Notice what the colour of this emotion is and if there are any stories attached to it. Notice if it feels heavy or light, and if it might have come from a certain area of your body. Imagine raising your hands up towards the sky, cupping this ball of energy and releasing it to the universe. Watch the ball of energy float up until it has dissipated completely. Feel a sense of release within your body.

You might want to repeat this a few times until you feel

the process is complete. After you have released everything that you felt called to release to the universe, imagine standing calm, peaceful and strong, looking out at the beautiful view. Imagine raising your arms up above your head and receiving love, luck and protection back from the cosmos.

Now place one hand on your heart and one hand on your tummy. Take a deep breath and feel back into your physical body, noting the placement of your hands in this time and space. Bring your awareness back to the sounds in the room and the feeling of the body comfortably on the floor. Bring a smile to your face and close the visualisation practice with a few deep breaths.

Raise your vibration

Did you know that musical vibrations have healing possibilities? Solfeggio frequencies are sound patterns that interact with your brain waves, autonomic nervous system and hormones, helping to make you feel calm. Listening to them can promote mental, emotional, physical and spiritual harmony and health and healing. Solfeggio frequencies date back to Gregorian chants by Benedictine monks and you can download them to listen to. Harvard studies, among others, have shown the healing possibilities of these frequencies and of music in general.

Take some time to search the internet for a 639 hertz track that you enjoy listening to – there are hundreds to choose from on YouTube. The frequency of 639 hertz is associated with harmonious relationships, and is said to help with the healing of close or collective relationships. Listening to this frequency will connect you to your heart chakra and facilitate a greater connection to the universe. Play your chosen Solfeggio frequencies track in the background as you work, play, eat, meditate or sleep this month, to aid with manifesting harmonious relationships.

A MEDITATIVE POEM

What if
we loved anyway
kept open
stayed soft
placed one foot in front of the other

What if
despite the world that moves around us
we breathed deep
into our heart
to open still

What if
we remembered
we're all trying our best
all getting it wrong
from time to time

What if
we concerned ourselves
only
with our own words and choices
and made them pure

What if
we become
the love we seek
what then
what if

A DEFLECTION SPELL

If you are experiencing negative energy from a person or people, you can use this spell to reverse any negativity you are receiving, deflecting it back to the giver. Please first think about if you truly know it is coming from an outside source, rather than your own limiting belief, energetic block or interpretation.

Placing a mirror in strategic positions (outside of your home, on your desk) or wearing a mirror as an amulet can be a powerful aid for deflection of negative energy. This is in no way black magic, as you will simply be protecting yourself from receiving negative energy and just returning it to where it came from. Perform this spell on a full moon.

You will need

Smudging stick
A small pocket mirror (that you don't normally use)
A small black candle

1. Begin by smudging the mirror, the space you are in and yourself. Settle and ground yourself with a few deep breaths.

2. Begin by lighting the candle in front of the mirror. Imagine a circle of protection around you – this invisible force field of light only lets in positive energy (and anything else out). Connect with the protection and support of the universe. Stay with this visualisation for a few minutes.

3. Feel a sense of compassion and good will – what does that feel like? Where in your body do you feel it? What colour might represent it? Notice how the feeling of compassion is maternal, strong and wise.

4. When you feel you are vibrating at the level of compassion and good will, open your eyes and take your gaze to the mirror for a few minutes, as if to charge the mirror with the feeling and intention.

5. Once you feel as if the mirror is sufficiently charged (your intuition will tell you), you can let go of the practice. Let the candle burn out on its own (you might need to do this spell a few times, so stub it out rather than blow it out in between spell sessions).

6. Once the candle has burned out, the mirror is charged. Place your mirror somewhere of significance, perhaps in your front garden, at your front door or on your desk at work. Leave it there until the next new moon, and then bury it somewhere safe.

Understand the law of polarity

The law of polarity states that there is always a positive to every negative. This can be extremely helpful when facing challenges in life or when experiencing conflict in relationships. The law of polarity and the law of attraction are, in many ways, two of a kind. If you wish to repair, strengthen or deepen a relationship, you have to be the magnet for it; you need to be your true self and not mask your true feelings. Then you will attract what works in perfect harmony with you. You must be the natural energy that flows within you and not try to be someone you are not.

September's practice

Morning

Start the day with a 5-minute meditation, listening to a 639-hz frequency track. Set a timer and light a candle or incense if you choose.

Next, place both hands over your heart and repeat some, or all, of the affirmations on page 164.

Write a list of three people you are grateful for, and why.

Evening

Practise the visualisation on page 170 before going to sleep.

10
SELF-ACCEPTANCE

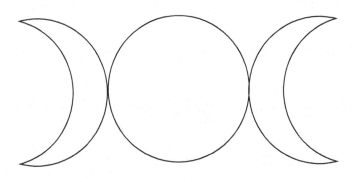

OCTOBER

'WHICH PART OF YOU REQUIRES
ACCEPTANCE AND WHICH PART OF
YOU GRANTS IT?'

Self-acceptance can sometimes feel like the trickiest pursuit of them all. Showing compassion and kindness to a best friend or child might come easy to you, but often showing yourself the same unconditional kindness and love is where some get stuck. Do you talk to yourself the same way you do to your best friend? Do you offer yourself the same compassion when you mess up or feel like you're struggling?

Self-acceptance is unconditional. It is different to self-esteem, which is tied to your sense of worth. Manifesting self-acceptance requires compassion and surrender. It is a process of softening that allows an integration of your whole self: your shadow, your inner child, your ego, your fear, your joy and your soul. I like to imagine self-acceptance as becoming the divine parent of ourselves living in a state of open awareness and gentle curiosity, fully present, accepting of self and life as it is. Self-acceptance is the ultimate love and is the process of truly mastering 'being and becoming'.

As the October trees shed their leaves in the northern hemisphere, spring flowers are beginning to bloom in the southern hemisphere. The falling leaves provide fertile ground for new shoots to bloom come spring. As the seasons move through a cycle of growth, bloom and letting go, each of us go through a similar cycle too. For women, the physical cycle is experienced and celebrated every month through menstruation. Energetically, mentally, emotionally and spiritually, our cycles of change are much longer, sometimes even by years. But there always comes a time to let go of the old in order to create fertile ground for the new to bloom.

Accepting yourself

You might see manifesting as drawing something from out there, closer into the here and now, but really it is the other way around. In order to manifest self-acceptance, you must relinquish all the 'yeah buts' or the 'haven't gots', and instead turn in, and trust yourself and the life that you are living.

Self-acceptance is about embracing your uniqueness, and knowing that you are here on this planet to evolve as a soul and as part of a collective consciousness. Self-acceptance doesn't require you to eliminate challenges, to never get triggered, feel sad or get things wrong – quite the opposite. Self-acceptance is about embracing and loving *all* aspects of yourself, as you continuously learn and evolve throughout life. Adopting an attitude of curiosity and compassion when you do get triggered is key. Getting triggered shows you what needs healing or tending to; it highlights whether your or other behaviours are out of alignment with your values; it indicates how present and regulated you are at any given moment. Adopting this attitude, you will be able to switch negative self-talk such as 'I'm so bad/broken/unworthy/rubbish', to 'Ooh, how interesting'. Failing at something shows that you tried! It is ultimately how we all learn.

As you begin to manifest deeper self-acceptance, it is helpful to consider which part of you requires acceptance and which part of you grants it. There is an awareness, a 'higher self' within us all, and that is the universe within. In order to trust yourself, you have to trust the universe. Surrendering to life is the path to self-acceptance and it is a path that leads to the truth that you are already enough.

Reflect on what you are ready to let go of, in order to manifest a greater sense of self-acceptance. Write each out on a piece of paper and write out what gifts those old beliefs might have brought you. For example: 'I am ready to let go of perfectionism. I thank that part of me for trying to keep me safe and for contributing to all I have achieved, but it is no longer serving me. With thanks, I choose now to let perfectionism go and to know I am good enough as I am.'

The gold within

In 1957, a giant clay Buddha statue was being relocated from a monastery in Thailand. A monk noticed a crack. For fear of damaging it, they set it back down to rest it for a while. Later that day, a monk came back to check on the statue. As he shone a flashlight over it he noticed something bright shining within. He started to chip away at the clay and revealed a gold buddha statue hidden beneath. It is believed that monks 200 years earlier had covered the statue with clay to protect it during a Burmese invasion. Tragically, all the monks were killed during the attack, so their hidden treasure remained lost.

This incredible story speaks of the gold hidden within each of us that we have covered with our fears. For you, this might be judgements, hatred, jealousy, bitterness or perception of events. In order to manifest more of anything in our lives, especially self-acceptance, we must gently and lovingly remove the outer layers of protection, just as the monks did in 1957 to reveal the statue of gold.

GET TO KNOW YOURSELF

Manifesting acceptance requires an energetic softening and the mental relinquishing of control in order to reveal the gold that lies within you.

Spend some time journaling your answers to these questions:

✧ What do you want?

✧ What is keeping you from embodying your true authentic expression?

✧ What are you holding on to that might be blocking you from experiencing self-acceptance? Is it thoughts, past experiences or fear of the unknown?

✧ What stories is your body telling you? Where are you holding tension and why might that be? Tension in your shoulders could mean holding the weight of the world, for example.

✧ When you feel stuck, anxious or stressed, what are you thinking and believing? What would the opposite thoughts and beliefs be?

✧ Where are you holding yourself prisoner in your own life? What would forgiving yourself give to you?

✧ What would self-acceptance feel and look like for you?

A JOURNEY TO SELF-ACCEPTANCE

As a young woman, Louise Harris was seemingly successful and healthy from the outside, but felt stressed and constantly compared herself with others. Her life simmered with a sense of anxiety and disconnection. In her external search for her identity, she viewed the world as separate to herself, and so the gap of self-acceptance edged wider and wider.

Louise now realises that her younger self was a perfectionist – striving to be more, all the time. For Louise, manifesting self-acceptance was a progressive journey that gradually evolved over time, and with practice. Now a yoga teacher and shamanic healer, Louise doesn't fear turning inward and is able to truly love what is, including herself, as a result. Connecting with a higher energy – or spirit, as Louise refers to it – through her shamanic work, was where her self-trust and acceptance really started to cement.

As she began to trust spirit, she was able to trust herself, and as this symbiotic relationship deepened, Louise noticed synchronicities occurring every single day. She found that trusting something bigger than herself *is* letting go of control, and it allowed her to trust that what is meant for her will show up.

Louise's manifesting practice isn't about striving for something specific (a sum of money, a flashy car . . .). Instead, her intention is to receive more of her gifts, to deepen her sense of purpose and to allow spirit to move through her in that way. Her daily meditation practice, breathwork, teaching yoga and group work helps her step into union with spirit, and the vibration of openness and trust, every day.

For Louise, being in a place of self-acceptance feels like a beautiful place to arrive, where life feels so much easier and more peaceful. She suggests that you just have to keep looking in. It may feel unfamiliar to start with, but after a while you realise that is the only place you'll find, accept, and truly love yourself.

Change your mind

Being self-critical doesn't mean you're broken or bad. In fact, it just means you are human. The unfortunate symptom of cognitive evolution – a.k.a. the ego mind – is a tendency to be overanalytical. It was all part of a survival strategy and served a very useful function in the days when it was necessary. Understanding the two aspects of our internal experience – the ego mind and the universal mind (as explored further in November's chapter) – is essential for manifesting deeper self-acceptance. By its very nature, self-acceptance requires you to accept all of you. When you go to war with the ego and label it as bad and unwanted, you are creating resistance within yourself, going to war with, and rejecting and disowning parts of yourself. Meditation and mindfulness practices have been linked to the increased ability to be self-compassionate and self-forgiving.

Developing the skill of being able to see yourself and your experiences from the seat of awareness, which mindfulness and meditation facilitate, allows you to cultivate the habit of being fully present to what is and to love and accept yourself as you are. A teacher of mine used to say that we are always trusting something – either we are trusting the voice of fear or ego, or we are trusting our intuition or higher self. Trusting the universe within is the key that will unlock self-acceptance.

What if you believed you are enough? What if you let go of trying to control all the external parts around you? What if you let go of the past? What if you believe you are supported? What if you forgave yourself? What if you lifted the lid on the dreams you have for yourself and your life and knew you deserved them all?

AFFIRMATIONS FOR SELF-ACCEPTANCE

Repeat the following affirmations:

✧ I accept myself as I am

✧ I am already enough

✧ I choose to forgive myself and others

✧ I am welcome, safe, loved and protected

✧ I give myself permission to experience peace

✧ The more peaceful I feel within, the more peace surrounds me

✧ I am proud of who I am

✧ What is meant for me will not pass me by

Cacao ritual for inner peace

Do this ritual in the evening of a full moon. Ashwagandha is a herb used in Ayurveda, and people have used it for thousands of years to relieve stress, increase energy levels and improve concentration. You are going to make a delicious, warming drink – perfect for a cool autumnal evening.

You will need

Smudging stick
A white candle
A saucepan and small whisk
1 cup almond, coconut or oak mylk
1½ tbsp raw organic cacao
Your favourite cup
4 fresh mint leaves
½ tsp dried ashwagandha
1 tsp honey or maple syrup

1. Smudge the space you are in, and yourself. Light your candle and set the intention to be focused and present for the ritual.

2. Begin heating the mylk in the saucepan, in a meditative state. Gently whisk in the cacao and say: 'I connect with my heart and allow love to be my essence.'

3. Next, gently stir in the ashwagandha and declare: 'I let go of any stress, anxiety or tension in my mind, body, heart and soul. I choose to feel good now.'

4. Next, stir in the honey or maple syrup and say: 'I remember the sweetness of this precious life and the gift of every unfolding moment. I honour the sweetness within me.'

5. Add the mint leaves and say: 'I allow myself to have a fresh perspective. I cleanse my mind of any negativity.'

6. Pour the mixture into your favourite cup and take a seat, either on the floor or chair. Hold the cup with both hands, close to your heart and say: 'I bless this brew with harmony and balance, let it nourish me and reconnect me to my calm, compassionate, loving essence. Thank you, thank you, thank you.'

7. With your eyes closed, and in a meditative state, take your time to slowly sip, savour and enjoy your brew. Take your time.

8. Once you have finished, rub your palms together to create some heat between your hands. Gently place your palms over your eyes. Open your eyes behind the darkness. Take a deep breath and slowly peel your hands away, letting in a little bit of light, imagining seeing with clearer, fresh new eyes.

9. Safely stub your candle out.

☾ ☾ ☾ ○

CHOOSE A SYMBOL
FOR THIS MONTH

Most symbols for self-acceptance involve a process or a journey of some sort, and often one that involves moving through challenges. When considering the symbolism of myths and fables, this journey towards transformation is depicted beautifully as 'the hero/heroine's journey'.

No matter where you are on your own journey, choose a symbol this month that resonates deeply with your own personal hero/heroine's journey. You can choose from one of the symbols listed below or ask the universe for a clear sign.

THE LOTUS FLOWER

A poetic symbol for inner peace, strength and rebirth. The lotus flower grows in the mud and darkness and later blooms on the surface as a beautiful, clean, vibrant flower. The popular phrase 'no mud, no lotus' symbolises that the journey of life is made up of darkness and light, and we require challenges in order for us to bloom.

UNALOME

The Buddhist symbol for inner peace. With its twists and turns, this spiral symbol represents the journey through life, towards inner peace and enlightenment.

TRIPLE MOON

This symbol illustrates a full moon, with a waxing and waning moon either side. This is a pagan symbol for femininity. Sometimes referred to as the 'triple goddess', it represents the past, present and future as a journey through life.

DARA KNOT

The Celtic dara knot symbolises self-acceptance and wisdom. Dara translates to 'oak', and the entangled knot-like symbols represent the roots of a sacred oak tree that hold and support the magnitude of the visible tree above.

TREE OF LIFE

Also a Celtic symbol, the tree of life represents the relationship between the inner and outer world. It also represents strength, beauty, uniqueness and longevity.

Embody the vibration of trust

I have learned that embodying the vibration of trust and surrender is where the magic really takes place. My own ever-evolving journey of manifesting self-acceptance has been long and revealing. In the beginning, repairing the rupture of self-love often felt like there was too much work to do, and that I had too far to go. Any attempts I'd make at understanding self-acceptance felt as if I was swimming upstream, not getting anywhere at all. It wasn't until my physical body put the brakes on, and I was forced to surrender.

I realised that it was surrender, and trusting myself to the flow of my life, that led me to my desires – not effort and force. They were, and are, all waiting downstream for me in the path of least resistance. When you let go, you become vibrationally free of resistance, and so then naturally become more magnetic. Ask yourself these questions:

✧ Where in your life does it feel like you're swimming upstream?

✧ Are there any parts of your life that you are seeking to control or stay in control of?

✧ Is there room for you to relax and let go, and trust the flow of life that will carry you?

When you feel tension, resistance or effort to control creep in this month, yield. Your vibration will effortlessly shift every time you soften and trust the flow – nothing for you to do, to force or bring about, but instead just to *allow*. You've got this.

A MEDITATIVE POEM

and then I surrendered
freed myself from the burden of trying
to be more than I am
let go of striving
to be . . . just that little bit more
I sunk my roots deep
felt into the abundance that already surrounds me
and gasped for air
as if waking in a dream
breathing
for the first time in a while
I arrived home
in this body
exactly as I am

Select a talisman

You are going to select a keepsake this month to remind you of your self-worth and of your intention for self-acceptance. When you reflect on it, it will help to evoke feelings of gratitude, hope and self-connection.

1. Take some time to reflect on the last decade, or more, and write down three experiences or achievements that you are most proud of, and why.

2. Next, take a look at your list to see if one jumps out at you that could be represented in a tangible object. This might be a photograph of your children, a plane ticket or a thank you card . . . this will be your talisman for this month.

3. Once you have selected your talisman, anoint it with feeling gratitude, before displaying it somewhere you'll see regularly (on your desk or in your work space, for example).

4. Make it a small ritual to spend a few moments each day looking at or holding your talisman. Every time it catches your attention, let your talisman remind you of the strength, passion and commitment you have within you.

Understand the law of perpetual transmutation

The eighth law of the universe, the law of perpetual transmutation, suggests that you can't manifest your desires unless you embrace change and let go of control. The law states that energy is always transforming and changing shape. It forms the bedrock for the notion that your thoughts become things, simply because the law states that energy manifests into experiences. It is our intention and focus that decide what those will be.

This law teaches us that it is important to maintain

consistency, because intentions that are scattered and uncertain will only manifest themselves as chaotic half measures of what we are asking for. In a practical sense, this law gives us a tangible process to work through our emotions in order to experience better self-acceptance because it gives us something to do with tricky emotions – namely, turn them into something else. A challenging experience could be transmuted into a beautiful poem or a song, for example. You are an energetic being; therefore, you are an expression of this law, always changing, always evolving.

October's practice

Inspired by Louise Hay's book, *You Can Heal Your Life* (1984), this month you are going to look in the mirror and be kind to yourself. I remember the first time I stood in front of a mirror, looked myself in the eye, and said 'I love you'. I was at my best friend's house and we took it in turns to try. It felt CRINGEY, uncomfortable, untrue, laughable and downright stupid. As I showed up more, I moved through various stages of deep emotion before slowly starting to feel more comfortable, until eventually I meant it. So, this month, have a go!

Morning

Every morning before your day begins, go to the bathroom mirror, take a deep breath, look yourself in the eye and say: 'I love you, I accept you, I am proud of you, I love you.'

Evening

Grab your journal before bed and journal your answers to these four questions:

✧ What did you learn about myself today?

✧ What can you let go of from today?

✧ What did you learn about the world today?

✧ What is your intention for tomorrow?

11

INTUITION

NOVEMBER

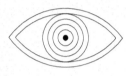

'INTUITION REALLY IS A
MAGICAL POWER'

Most of us have experienced intuition at some point in our lives, perhaps experienced as a hunch, a feeling that something wasn't quite right, or an instinctual response to something actioned without thinking. Intuition is your inner compass, a gut-feeling guidance system, often sensed without logical reasoning. Intuition is often referred to as the inner voice, one heard through sensations, signs and images rather than necessarily with words. Ancient cultures revered intuition as sacred and vital, whereas Western cultures tend to dismiss it in favour of the logical mind. I think both intuition and logic should be integrated and incorporated in our experiences. Intuition itself really is a magical power.

This month we are going to celebrate and honour the unseen, and intuitive guidance. As light gives way to darkness in the northern hemisphere, the southern hemisphere once again welcomes the return of lighter, longer days. This seasonal transition from light to dark, dark to light is a potent time when the veil between worlds is said to be thin. The pagan festival of Samhain, celebrated on the transition from 31 October into 1 November, inspired the globally popularised celebration of Halloween. The 'veil being thin' simply refers to the separation between the material and the spiritual worlds, light and dark, and the conscious and unconscious mind.

Dia de los Muertos (Day of the Dead) is celebrated in Mexico, and by people around the world, on 1 and 2 November, and is a festival honouring the unseen, and life and death (see page 199).

ANIMAL INSTINCT

Instinct is associated with an animalistic survival mechanism innate within us all. Intuition is associated with higher levels of consciousness and the ability to tap into the collective consciousness. Both instinct and intuition are intrinsically interlinked. It is easy to recognise instinct in our animal friends, and we tend to forget that we are mammals just like them. During the catastrophic Indian Ocean tsunami on Boxing Day in 2004, animals were seen moving inland before the tsunami struck. According to a BBC report, elephants, flamingos, cats, dogs and buffalo all fled for higher ground. Some survivors recognised their warning and ran along with them.

A sixth sense

Your intuition might guide you in a practical, instinctual way to keep you from danger – for example, offering a gut feeling to not take a certain route home or to change your plans without a logical reason. It will also guide you in more mystical ways, to make soul-aligned decisions in your life. Many successful business people, scientists, medical professionals, artists, creators and healers attribute their decision-making and success to intuition. Where exactly this voice of inner knowing comes from is widely debated – a higher intelligence, the soul, spirit guides, universal mind/collective consciousness, animal instinct or precognition; nobody can agree.

Precognition is a term given to explain the extrasensory ability to see or sense events or occurrences from another time or before they have happened; it is your sixth sense. Some people experience this through their dreams, synchronicities, feelings, visions, or through a feeling of déjà vu. Perhaps you've had the experience where you've thought of someone and suddenly they call or text saying they were thinking of you too?

This month you will focus on developing your own sense of intuition and connection to the collective consciousness. Being able to hear and trust your own intuition will be rocket fuel for your manifesting practice. You can see your intuition as your inner compass, and your manifesting practices as the fuel that will propel you forward.

DAY OF THE DEAD

Day of the Dead, on 1 and 2 November, is a time to honour your ancestors. This might be done simply through quiet reflection, prayer, looking through old family photo albums, visiting sacred sites, or by lighting a candle and placing it in your window to honour souls who have passed and all those yet to come. Sometimes we receive guidance via intuitive sensing from loved ones, past and present, and this practice will open your intuition up to receiving.

GET TO KNOW (BEYOND) YOURSELF

To understand collective consciousness (or the universal mind, as it is sometimes referred to) is to understand intuition. Sometimes you have experiences that you just can't explain. Perhaps you know something about someone before they tell you, or you dream about something before it happens. Trusting your inner guidance system is essential for any manifesting practice. You must recognise synchronicities when they appear, take action, and say yes when the path is presented before you.

There are a number of blocks which could prevent you from hearing and trusting your own intuitive responses. Perhaps it's fear of what other people would think of you, an old belief that it is just woo-woo nonsense. Perhaps it's a fear of the unknown or simply a muscle that hasn't yet truly been flexed.

Spend some time exploring what might be blocking you from connecting to your own intuition. Think about when your intuition has supported you by journaling your responses to the following questions throughout this month:

◇ What stories have I been told about intuition or psychic abilities?

◇ When have I felt connected to my intuition?

◇ Why is connecting deeper to my intuition important to me?

◇ Have I ever experienced my sixth sense? How does it feel?

A STORY OF INTUITION

Small business owner and creative, Bobbi Brown was waiting to board a minibus in a remote village in Senegal, West Africa, when a strange feeling surged through her. Unable to translate the feeling at the time, she mistook it for anxiety. Her rational mind convinced her to ignore it, because it was the last bus, and she and her boyfriend wanted to get home. So they clambered on board the packed 'car rapide' and found a seat. Half an hour into the journey, the feeling Bobbi was experiencing started to rise and overwhelm her. Her boyfriend suggested they get off the bus but Bobbi tried to rationalise staying on; she didn't want to cause a fuss and they were in the middle of nowhere. But her boyfriend, who was Senegalese, and of a culture that honours intuition, insisted that they listen to her gut feeling, and called out to the bus driver to pull over. A little embarrassed, yet with an overwhelming sensation of relief, Bobbi disembarked with her boyfriend and bags, and watched the minibus pull away. They stood, wondering what on earth they were going to do next, when they heard a loud explosion. The minibus, about 100 metres down the road, had lost a tire and crashed. They raced to help. Bobbi realised the two passengers she had been sitting next to were badly injured and her now vacant seat was the seat directly above the wheel arch. Her intuition had saved them.

Bobbi admitted to me that she felt confused by the experience at the time, realising now that we in the West don't really have the language to describe such events, and stories such as this are often dismissed as unbelievable. Yet, to those she shared the experience with in Senegal, who have a different collective belief system, it was very much celebrated as a moment of intuitive guidance.

Change your mind

Understanding the two levels of mind – the collective consciousness (or universal mind), and the individual mind (or the ego) – is the key to unlock greater access in your intuition. The individual mind uses words or thoughts, whereas intuition uses a deeper sensing. The individual mind is concerned with what it can experience through the five senses; the universal mind is concerned with the sixth sense and the energy field that connects everything in the universe. The individual mind is the 'conscious' mind that labels, analyses, judges and rationalises, whereas the universal mind, or collective consciousness, involves the unconscious mind, and so is usually only experienced through this sensing. This is not to say that the rational mind should be ignored – not at all – just that intuition should be in balance in our decision-making and experiences, but just as a true healer utilises specific knowledge alongside their intuition.

I saw the movie *Top Gun: Maverick* recently and was thrilled to hear the lead character, played by Tom Cruise, repeatedly advise the trainee pilots, who were making decisions in highly challenging situations: 'Don't think, just do.' The instruction suggests that they are better off trusting their intuitive wisdom, rather than their thinking mind. Manifesting from the seat of intuition requires you to do exactly that – don't think, just do. To accomplish this, you must embody the concept of being rather than doing.

AFFIRMATIONS FOR SELF-ACCEPTANCE

Use these following affirmations to connect to your intuition:

- ✧ I am divinely guided
- ✧ I am open to receiving divine guidance
- ✧ I trust my intuition to guide the way
- ✧ I am supported by the universe
- ✧ I recognise signs and synchronicities as messages from the universe
- ✧ I am never alone

✧ An intuition writing ✧ ritual

Stream-of-consciousness journaling is a powerful tool to access your intuition. The practice was made popular in *The Artist's Way* (1992), where author Julia Cameron instructs her readers to write a three-page brain dump of thoughts each morning – 'morning pages'. The book inspired many other authors and spiritual teachers to develop their own version of the practice, sometimes referred to as psychography or automatic writing. I've practised my own form of this for many years called 'Dear Universe', which is now well over 60,000 words, and I often turn to it for intuitive guidance. With regular practice you will find that you are able to access guidance from your higher self, and it can be incredibly reassuring and insightful. Do this practice first thing in the morning or last thing at night.

You will need

Smudging stick
A white candle
A timer
A notebook and pen

1. Set up your space by smudging it with a smudging stick. Light the candle. Practise a 5-minute meditation to consciously settle the mind to help you access the theta brain wave state (low and slow brain waves that occur when relaxed, see page 209).

When you are ready, set a timer for 10 minutes.

2. Pick up your notebook and invite your intuitive self to step forward. Write out a question or something you would like guidance for on a page in your journal. Address the question to your intuition, or to

the universe as I do, or simply write the question. Without time to think, start to write a response as a stream of consciousness.

3. You might find that you are writing from the thinking mind to begin with, such as: 'I'm not sure how to answer this, I guess . . .' Just keep writing, without pausing for thought or reflection. You might find that you need to ask another question to dig deeper: 'What do I mean by this?' or, simply, 'Why?' Through a stream of consciousness, allow intuitive responses to come. Keep writing until the timer has sounded and not before.

4. You may find that you want to continue, in which case do so until you feel like coming to a natural close.

5. When you are ready to stop, place the pen down, take a few deep breaths and whisper 'thank you, thank you, thank you' before taking a moment of reflection. You might like to read over the writing and take away an intuitive insight. When you are ready to close the ritual, take one more deep breath and stub the candle out.

CCC O

CHOOSE A SYMBOL
FOR THIS MONTH

The universe communicates to us in symbols and signs, or 'spirit winks', as Janet Conner puts it in her fantastic book *The Lotus and the Lily* (2012). Each of us has our own personal 'spirit wink' which can change over time. For me it is seeing a heart shape or a butterfly, and both have shown up at the most synchronistic of times and in the most unlikely of places. And when they do, the amount of relief, guidance and magic I feel never ceases to amaze me. For my best friend, it is a sun symbol, and for others I've known, it is feathers, robins, dandelion seeds, coins and yellow cars, to name but a few! Only you and your intuition can decide what your sign is. If you don't know, ask for a sign that is so clear you can't miss it this month. Then remain present and aware so you notice it when it shows up.

WHITE FEATHER

A white feather is a sign from the universe that your prayers and requests are being answered. For angel experts, a white feather is a sign that someone from the spirit world is looking out for you. Even though they are not physically here on this earth anymore, they want you to know that you are supported, and to have hope.

1111

1111 is associated with intuition, creativity and alignment, and is the most recognised numerical sign from the universe. When you see 1111 it means you are on the right track and are being divinely guided.

ROBIN

Robins, and other birds, are commonly seen as a sign from the universe or angels. It could be a sign from a loved one to keep the faith and to know you are loved, or to follow your intuition to lead you along the right path.

Visualise this

There are four different types of communication within the psychic realm: clairvoyance (seeing), clairaudience (hearing), clairsentience (feeling) and claircognizance (knowing). Clairvoyant messages appear as images, visions and scenes, often as metaphors or indications of past, present or future events. Such messages or metaphors can also be received by some people by tuning in with objects. No matter the method, all require one thing: to tune in.

This month practise the art of allowing a visualisation to come to you, rather than actively creating the visualisation in your mind. You can practise this in a number of ways:

✧ After you are settled into a meditation and are comfortably in a relaxed state (not in a thinking-mind state), allow yourself to daydream. Make a note of the images, visions or symbols that come.

✧ All objects hold energy of their own and can be the transmitter for intuitive messages. Hold an object, a photograph or something tangible in your hands, and tune in to the story and energy that it holds.

✧ Pay particular attention to dreams. You might like to keep a dream journal as instructed on page 63.

Raise your vibration

Your brain and intuition are intrinsically linked. The more relaxed the mind is, the more open it is to receiving intuitive information. There are five types of brain waves, ranging from gamma (the fastest, shallowest brain wave, responsible for focus, memory and learning) to delta (a slower, deeper wave frequency achieved during deep sleep). These frequencies are measured by scientists and doctors using EEG (electroencephalogram) machines.

When you are in the fast brain wave frequencies – busy thinking – it is near impossible to manifest your desires. Relaxing into the slower brain wave frequencies is where the manifesting magic takes place. Theta brain waves occur during meditation, light sleep, deep relaxation and dreaming, a state seen as the portal between the thinking mind and the collective consciousness. It is in the theta brain wave state that your manifestation practice is most effective. Intuition, however, is always communicating to you, whatever brain wave state you are in, if you're present enough to recognise it.

Take time every day to consciously and intentionally raise your vibration by entering into a theta brain wave state. You do this through meditation and relaxed visualisation, and this, in turn, helps you plug in to the universal mind. The more practiced you are at this, the clearer you will be able to recognise your intuition throughout your waking life.

A MEDITATION TO ACTIVATE YOUR INTUITION

Get into a comfortable upright position. Close your eyes and take a few rounds of deep breaths. Set a timer for 10 minutes.

Set the intention to be present for the remainder of the meditation. Consciously relax your face muscles, shoulders, belly, hips, arms, hands and legs.

Take your awareness up to the middle of your forehead, just above the space between your eyebrows. Imagine the colour indigo circling or filling this space, or imagine the energy of this space opening like petals from a flower. You might experience a tingle or sensation of heat, simply by taking your awareness there. You are activating your third eye, the chakra associated with intuition, clarity and the ability to truly 'see'.

You might like to repeat some of the affirmations found on page 204 silently in your mind. Keep your focus on the third eye, if you can.

When the timer sounds, take a deep breath and raise your arms wide above your head, reaching out to the universe. Draw your hands back down in a prayer position to your heart and close your meditation with a deep breath.

Gather your tools

Use the following crystals, herbs, woods and tools as talismans and symbols to remember your intention to activate your intuition through this month:

Crystal: Apophyllite
Colour: Indigo
Essential oil: Bergamot
Chakra: Third eye
Herb: Mugwort
Animal totem: Wolf
Wood: Alder
Candle colour: Indigo

Understand the law of oneness

The universal law of oneness states that everything in this universe, seen or unseen, is connected. Through collective consciousness, or the universal mind, the law of oneness binds humanity, the planet and the cosmos. This law is infinite in space, time and energy. Everything in the universe is energy and made up of the same stuff, including you. Listening to your intuition is to allow the flow of communication between your conscious mind and the universal mind. You might hear spiritual explorers saying 'you are made of stardust', and on a subatomic level this is true. The law of oneness suggests that what we do has an impact on the whole, not just for us as an individual, and so everything you manifest has an impact on the world and someone else. Energy cannot be created or destroyed, only transformed, which explains psychic intuitive guidance. Our thinking mind, or our ego, is what makes us believe all things are separate and that we live in a dualistic world, but on a deeper level we are all one – something your intuition knows all about.

November's practice

Allowing your intuitive wisdom to be heard is not something you can force or really 'work on', but rather, something you surrender to. Your inner compass is already active and communicating with you; your job is to get quiet enough to listen and to trust the sense of knowing when it does pour though. The process of surrender may take time and practice, so keep it simple: meditate, spend time in nature and trust yourself. You are your own best teacher and all the answers you seek are within.

Morning

Light a candle to signify the beginning of your morning ritual. Say a few words of gratitude for the day. Set the intention to be present and notice any signs or 'spirit winks' and invite them in.

Set a timer for 10 minutes. As you meditate, consciously connect in with the sounds around you, including your breath. Focus on taking your awareness to your heart.

Any time when needed

Take a mindful walk in nature, without digital distractions. Either go alone or make an agreement with those you are walking with to spend some time in silence.

12

A BETTER WORLD

DECEMBER

'TO MANIFEST A BETTER WORLD, WE MUST REMEMBER THE ANCIENT WISDOM OUR ANCESTORS ONCE EMBODIED'

Somehow, during the insanity of colonialism and the rise of the patriarchy, people have lost their sense of connection with the planet – our home – and with each other. Modern society has forgotten how to live in harmony with nature and the seasons, and in tune with their bodies and their intuition. We have forgotten to believe in magic.

Manifesting a better world requires the collective view of the world to shift and a new paradigm to be created, something which ultimately begins with each individual – you! Most of us have agency over how lightly we tread, how kindly we act, or how destructively or regeneratively we live. All of us have agency over our own minds. Advances in collective consciousness, evident throughout history, move in a similar way to a wave – drawing backward slightly before surging forward.

The power of individuals who have embodied peace in their lifetimes and subsequently manifested monumental changes in societal reordering is evident. Nelson Mandela's ability to master inner peace and embody love, forgiveness and compassion when unjustly incarcerated for 20 years contributed significantly to the end of the apartheid in South Africa. Mother Teresa gave a life of service to those in need; Shirin Ebadi peacefully fought for women's rights in Iran; the Dalai Lama continues to promote a message of non-violence; Mahatma Gandhi inspired Indians to choose non-violence in reclaiming their independence; and the essential teachings of Buddha and Jesus need little introduction. One of the most important movements of our modern time is the Black Lives Matter movement, which gained global attention after the tragic murder of George Floyd in 2020.

Collective belief systems, made up of individuals' thoughts, attention, energy and actions, must be directed towards creating a just, kind and fair world for *all* of humanity, a humanity that remembers how to live in harmony with the ecosystem we are a part of.

To manifest a better world, we must remember the ancient wisdom our ancestors once embodied, lost in the chaos, noise and separation of the modern world. As individuals we must embody generosity, to live aligned and on purpose, to take peaceful action to *be* love, and to intrinsically grasp the law of oneness (page 211). To manifest a better world, we have to start asking: 'How can I be of service?', rather than, 'What can I get?'

As we move towards the end of the year, with festivities taking place across the world, it is a perfect time to do what the Celts did best – celebrate! Winter solstice occurs in the northern hemisphere on 21 or 22 December each year, and marks the shortest day of the year. It is a perfect time to gather with your community and give thanks to this beautiful planet. Whether you choose to gather at a sacred site to honour the earth, skinny-dip under moonlight to honour divine feminine energy or dance around fire as the sun is setting to honour divine masculine energy, see solstice as an opportunity to pause, honour and give thanks to Mother Earth and the cyclical nature of all things. Manifesting a better world starts with honouring and appreciating this beautiful world, and seeing it all as sacred. The solstice is a perfect time to pause and do just this.

GET TO KNOW YOURSELF

To manifest a better world, we need to place all of humanity at the centre of our intention. This includes the life and health of Mother Earth. Spend some time journaling your responses to the following questions this month:

✧ What kind of world am I manifesting currently, through my thoughts, beliefs, behaviour and actions?

✧ What are my hopes for the natural world? And what are my current contributions towards achieving this?

✧ What are my hopes for humanity? And what are my current contributions towards achieving this?

✧ What are my hopes for the next generation, my children, grandchildren and the world they get to live in? And what are my current contributions towards this?

✧ What am I holding on to – emotionally, psychologically, energetically – that blocks me from extending compassion to all?

✧ What emotions do I feel when I think about the natural world and humanity?

✧ Where do I feel hope, love, compassion and optimism in my body? What colour would I associate with each and how can I cultivate more of each in my life?

A STORY OF STUBBORN OPTIMISM

Matt Hocking founded his B Corp–certified design agency, Leap, in 2004. A B Corp is a business that balances profit with people and the planet. Matt lives by a personal motto of 'stubborn optimism' and is undoubtedly manifesting many positive changes for the world through his work. He believes that just because we are told stories about the way the world is – 'humanity has always done this' and 'civilisation has always done that' – it doesn't have to be that way. For Matt, manifesting a better world means moving away from a capitalist, extractive economy towards a regenerative economy, where we remember we – humanity – are one small constituent of a much larger, older and ever-evolving ecosystem.

Despite his stubborn optimism, Matt also believes that we need to balance hope with realism. We might want the world to be perfect, but he reminds us that everything is perfectly imperfect – it is the essence of nature to be this way. On his peaceful mission, Matt admits he looks for signs and trusts his gut instinct, seeing them all as threads of curiosity to follow. For example, he sees three as a magic number and pays particular attention when two of something has come up, and then curiously awaits the third. He stays motivated and connected to his stubborn optimism approach through a daily gratitude practice, where he gives thanks to the natural world. He generally thanks nature and the universe in all ways, and his affirmation is: 'Thank you for today, thank you for all the days to come and all the days that have gone before, and thank you for now.' Then he asks: 'How can I be of service today?'.

Change your mind

The world is full of beauty, love, magic, community and kindness, and always has been, yet it is very easy to look at the state of the world portrayed by the media, the destruction being caused to the natural world, and the deprivation or separation evident in your own community, and feel overwhelmed. It is understandable to feel despondent and perhaps wonder what difference you, as one person, can really make.

If you constantly absorb the negative narrative that humanity is bad and there is no hope, or you spend all day watching the news, which is specifically designed to shock and incite fear, you will live in a state of fear, stress and anxiety. Fear is a block to manifesting your true desires for yourself and the world, and the negative effects of stress and anxiety on our mental, physical and emotional health is science-backed. By consuming lots of negative media, you are accidentally contributing to the perpetuating motion of negativity, the very thing you are wagging your finger at, wishing *it* would change.

It is an act of defiance to choose love instead. To see injustice as a call to take peaceful action, just as Nelson Mandela did. It is an act of defiance to not become despondent in the face of suffering, just as Mother Teresa demonstrated. It is an act of contribution to make every interaction you have, every choice you make, altruistic and fair. Evolution takes time, but you get to decide your contribution today.

AFFIRMATIONS FOR CHANGE

Empower yourself with these affirmations:

- ✧ Peace and harmony begins with me
- ✧ As I heal, the planet heals
- ✧ My choices, thoughts, words and behaviours impact the world
- ✧ I choose to make my choices healthy, loving and peaceful
- ✧ I choose to see this day as sacred
- ✧ Nature is my home
- ✧ How can I be of service today?
- ✧ Thank you for this beautiful world

Ritual to honour the earth

Pagan rituals, just as with those of many indigenous cultures, aim to attune us to nature and induce magic. They are often used to celebrate rites of passage, to honour the sacred and bring people together. This ritual is ideal for uniting your community; it can also be performed alone. It might be extra fun to perform this ritual with children.

You will need

A bonfire or outdoor fire pit to represent fire (or a candle)
A cup of salt
Two items that represent earth and air to you (take your time to choose – it might be a stone and a feather, for example)
A fresh glass of water (per person)
A piece of cake or something delicious to eat

1. This ritual should be performed outside. Take time and careful consideration to set up the space for this ritual, ensuring any fire you create is contained and safe.

2. Draw a protective circle around the space you are working in with a sprinkle of salt, or just in your mind's eye. In pagan tradition, this is done to protect you while the spell is being cast and to create a clear boundary between the physical world and the world of magic. Place your two items within your sacred circle. When you are all set up, the fire has been lit and you are all present, centred and ready to go, step into the circle.

3. First, spend some time in quiet reflection or meditation, feeling into your connection with Mother Earth. Listen to any natural sounds around you as you allow yourself to become present.

4. Hold the item that represents earth in your hands and offer deep gratitude to it. You might like to whisper words of prayer and thanks, or reflect on the miracle of the life-giving, life-sustaining earth, before placing the item down.

5. Next, pick up the item that represents air and do the same.

6. Now pick up your glass/es of water and spend some time in quiet reflection, feeling a deep sense of gratitude, whispering prayers of thanks before mindfully sipping and receiving the water.

7. Next, take your awareness to the fire and give a deep sense of gratitude for the light and warmth it brings. Allow yourself to become entranced by the magic of the flames and the dance of energy visual to you.

8. Next, place your hands somewhere on your body and offer a sense of gratitude to your perfect, living, miraculous human body.

9. Finally, turn your palms up towards the sky, or, if with others, hold hands forming a circle and tilt your faces up towards the sky. Offer a deep sense of gratitude to the stars, the cosmos and the magic of the universe and whisper prayers of gratitude and thanks.

10. Close the ritual with celebration! You might like to dance, sing, drum . . . whatever feels right for you (and your group). When the ritual has come to a close, dismantle the circle carefully and safely extinguish any fire.

$$(((\bigcirc$$

CHOOSE A SYMBOL
FOR THIS MONTH

When astronauts are able to view the whole
world as one from space, they frequently report a
significant cognitive shift. This phenomenon has
been given the official term 'the overview effect',
in which a heightened state of awe results in
significant personal and spiritual transformation.
With this in mind, the symbol of the Earth itself
might be enough to inspire a shift towards a
greater sense of love, respect and connection to
life itself – or you might like to select an option
from the list below. Either way, choose a symbol
for this month that inspires and uplifts you, and
helps you to feel connected to your global
community and the natural world.

MISTLETOE

Mistletoe is a symbol of peace, hope, fertility and resilience. The tradition of kissing under mistletoe at Christmas originated from the Celtic people of pre-Roman Britain; they also hung mistletoe in homes to ward off bad spirits and negative energy. Scandinavian countries have a slightly altered variation of this tradition, whereby standing under mistletoe symbolises a truce between friends, and past quarrels are surrendered by lovers with a kiss.

DOVES

The dove is a symbol of peace that spans many religions and cultures, making it one of the most internationally recognised symbols for peace. Native Americans believed the dove to be the deliverance of the great spirit and to symbolise peace, hope and love.

AN OLIVE BRANCH

Usually carried by a dove, the olive branch as a symbol for peace originates from Greek mythology and the Bible. Olive trees take a long time to grow, so are considered to be a tree only grown in peaceful times, not during times of war. The saying 'to hold out an olive branch' is used when describing the act of reaching out to someone to end a disagreement or to call a truce.

THE PEACE, OR 'V', HAND SIGN

The 'V' hand sign, created by the index finger and middle finger, first stood for victory during World War II. It was later adopted by anti-war protesters during the Vietnam War and is widely recognised today as a peace sign.

PEACE SIGN

The peace sign was originally designed by a British campaigner, Gerald Holtom, for the group Campaign for Nuclear Disarmament in 1958. It was later used by other anti-war and anti-nuclear groups in America and around the world. Today it is widely recognised and adopted as a sign for peace.

Visualise a kinder world

A 'loving kindness' meditation is a traditional Buddhist practice to cultivate compassion, kindness and love towards others. The idea is to extend kindness and compassion to someone you love, or an acquaintance or a stranger, or even someone you have difficult feelings towards. It could also be to the whole of creation. To practise this meditation, head to page 228.

Research is proving that this form of meditation increases feelings of compassion and altruism towards others. A study published in 2021 by the *International Journal of Environmental Research and Public Health* involved investigating the impact of loving kindness meditation on doctor – patient relationships. Their results showed that the group that had participated in regular loving kindness sessions demonstrated a significant increase in levels of compassion and empathy towards their patients, when compared to the control group that had not.

Raise your vibration

Meditating in a group is a magical experience, one that I personally love. It never fails to leave me feeling harmonised, uplifted and connected. The positive and tangible effects of group meditation have been the focus of numerous studies. Famously, a study carried out in New York saw a large group of meditators focus their intention on compassion and peace for the city. Their research found a 28 per cent reduction in the city's crime rate occurred during the experiment. Gathering in community to meditate for peace, for others, and for healing will not only raise your own vibration but also that of the planet. To raise your vibration this month, seek out a local meditation class or online meditation gathering to attend and enjoy.

LOVING KINDNESS MEDITATION

Set aside 10 to 15 minutes for this meditation. You might like to light a candle to signify the beginning of your meditation, and your intention to practise loving kindness while the flame is alight. You might also like to play some calming meditative music in the background or burn some incense.

Find a comfortable seated position and close your eyes. Take a few moments to settle your energy and relax your body before taking your awareness to your heart space and feeling the energy alive in your chest.

First, bring to mind someone you love unconditionally; it might be a child, a family member or a pet. Extend feelings of compassion, love and kindness to them, holding them in your mind's eye. Repeat the following affirmations:

✧ May you be well

✧ May you be safe

✧ May you find peace with whatever is happening

✧ May you accept yourself as you are

Then bring to mind a friend and repeat the exercise above, extending love and kindness to them and repeating the affirmations.

Next, bring to mind an acquaintance, someone you don't know particularly well, but recognise. This might be someone working in a local shop, a friend of a friend, or the person on the same train as you each morning. Extend loving kindness and repeat the affirmation above, directing it towards them.

Now bring to mind someone you have challenging feelings towards. Extend the same compassion and kindness to them through your intention and the affirmations, to the best of your ability. Now allow your awareness to extend out to all creation: the oceans, the skies, the trees, the birds and bees. Extend your loving kindness to all before drawing your awareness back to yourself. Place your hands over your heart and offer the same loving kindness to yourself, repeating the affirmations, replacing 'you' with 'I'.

Display a yuletide wreath

A wreath symbolises everlasting life and rebirth. Creating a wreath can be a mindfulness practice, or you could make one with your family or community as an act of celebration and to honour Mother Nature.

Wreaths were traditionally hung on the front door as a celebration, but also to attract the loving spirit of compassion into the home. Display your wreath on your door as an act of goodwill to all.

You could also choose to lay your wreath flat in your home, surrounding candles. Traditionally, wreaths included three purple candles, symbolising peace, hope and love. Whether you create a hanging wreath or a candle wreath, ideally it will be adorned with local foliage that acts as a celebration and gratitude for the season – evergreens in the northern hemisphere or spring/summer flowers in the southern hemisphere. Before its association with Advent, a wreath was a symbol of victory in ancient Greece and a symbol of a crown in Christianity. The circle represents everlasting life and eternity, with no beginning or end.

Understand the law of cause and effect

The universal law of cause and effect is very simple: every action produces a reaction. You may have learned a similar law in science class at school as one of Newton's laws, or recognise this as similar to the butterfly effect (see page 27). When we consider the law of cause and effect in our manifesting practice, we understand that every action, thought, word, choice and decision has an effect on our destiny, others and the planet. This may be seen as a burden at first glance, but it really is magic in motion! If you view yourself as the playful, powerful creator of your own experiences and the loving beneficiary of Mother Earth, you can start to change the causes – your thoughts or actions, for example – and fully appreciate or learn from the effects – what is manifesting around you. There is a famous quote often attributed to Lao Tzu:

Watch your thoughts; they become words. Watch your words; they become actions. Watch your actions; they become habits. Watch your habits; they become character. Watch your character; for it becomes your destiny. What we think, we become.

When you apply this law to the potential for collective change, you might feel the same sense of optimism as I do. Change is not only possible – it is inevitable.

December's practice

This month, focus on conscious or mindful consumerism, throughout your daily doings. Consider the journey, impact and regenerative opportunity of everything you purchase, whether that's gifts for others for Christmas, everyday items for yourself or the food you consume.

Let nothing go unthanked or unappreciated – up your gratitude practice for earthly gifts by thanking every glass of water and the food you consume for the life it sustains. Be thankful for everything, such as the shower you take – see it all as sacred.

Morning

Set your timer for 5-10 minutes and sit quietly in meditation to give thanks to the day, the earth and your body. Ask: 'How can I be of service today?'

Say the affirmations found on page 222 out loud or silently to yourself.

Evening

List in your journal three things you're grateful for, three things you learned about yourself and three things you learned about the world today.

REFERENCES

T. Morten Hansen, 'You Can Manage Luck. Here's How.' (Harvard Business Review www.hbr.org, 2011)

Richard Wiseman 'The Luck Factor' (*Skeptical Inquirer*, 2003)

Sophie Ekrod 'Efficacy of Acts of Kindness: examining effects on depressive symptoms and mental well-being and the mediating role of positive and negative emotions.' (University of Twente Student Theses, 2019)

Alyson L. Mahar, Virginie Cobigo & Heather Stuart 'Conceptualizing belonging' (*Disability and Rehabilitation*, 35:12 2013)

Daniel A. Yudkin, Annayah M. B. Prosser, S. Megan Heller (et al.) 'Prosocial correlates of transformative experiences at secular multi-day mass gatherings' (*Nature Communications* 12:2600, 2022)

Marianna Pogosyan 'The Health Benefits of Happiness' (Psychology Today psychologytoday.com, 2019)

Pamela Ebstyne King & Frederic Defoy 'Joy as a Virtue: The Means and Ends of Joy' (*BIOLA* 48:4, 2020)

Kris Putnam-Walkerly 'The Power of an Abundance Mindset for Changemakers' (*Leader & Leader* 99, 2021)

Alfredo Raglio, Lapo Attardo, Guilia Gontero (et al.) 'Effects of music and music therapy on mood in neurological patients' (*World Journal of Psychiatry* 5:1, 2015)

Nadine Gaab, Gottfried Shlaug, Lisa Wong 'Music as Medicine: The impact of healing harmonies' (The Longwood Seminars at Harvard Medical School, 2015)

Wei Xu. Marcus A. Rodriguez (et al.) 'The Mediating Effect of Self-Acceptance in the Relationship Between Mindfulness and Peace of Mind' (*Mindfulness* 6, 2015)

Hao Chen, Chao Liu, Xinyi Cao (et al.) 'Effects of Loving-Kindness Meditation on Doctors' Mindfulness, Empathy, and Communication Skills' (*International Journal of Environmental Research and Public Health* 18:8, 2021)

ACKNOWLEDGEMENTS

Thank you to you, the reader, for picking up this book and taking it into your life. I hope it helps you experience the magic, joy and love you deserve. I won't ever stop being grateful for the opportunity to write books, and the team at Ebury have been a dream to work with. An enormous thank you to Ru Merritt, Sam Heaton, Jessica Cselko, Becky Alexander, Meredith Olson, and the rest of the Ebury team, for being utterly brilliant. Thank you to my literary agent, Jane Graham-Maw, for her constant support and guidance. Thank you to my soul friends and family, especially Kirsten Baker, Ryan Chitty, Tia Tamblyn, Lucy O'Hagan and Nikki Hulin, for their unconditional love and support. With love and gratitude – thank you, thank you, thank you.

ABOUT THE AUTHOR

Joey Hulin is a meditation teacher, author and poet based in Cornwall who is making a name for herself as a thought leader in psychospiritual circles. She offers a down to earth, warm and playful approach to mindful living and spirituality. The founder of wellness company Horizon Inspired, she offers retreats, online courses and meditations around the world, creating nourishing opportunities for people to pause and reconnect. She can be found on Instagram at @joeyhulin_writer or at www.horizoninspired.co.uk.